# The ClearPath to Retirement

## Eliminate Obstacles & Create Efficiencies in Your Retirement Plan

Cory Zafke & Taylor Sundeen

This book discusses general concepts for retirement income planning and is not intended to provide tax or legal advice. Individuals are urged to consult with their tax and legal professionals regarding these issues.

The stories and characters in this book are fictional. Each story combines facts and circumstances redacted to highlight the subject matter of each chapter. Facts and circumstances are fictional and do not represent any one client in part or whole. They are included as an educational tool. No story should be treated to apply to the reader's individual circumstances. Always consult with your tax professional, attorney, and adviser before taking any action.

Investment advisory services are offered through Foundations Investment Advisors, LLC ("Foundations"), an SEC registered investment adviser. The content provided is intended for informational and educational purposes only. Additionally, the information contained herein does not constitute an offer to sell any securities or represent an express or implied opinion or endorsement of any specific investment opportunity, offering or issuer. Each individual investor's situation is different, and any ideas provided may not be appropriate for your particular circumstances. Foundations deems reliable any statistical data or information obtained from or prepared by third party sources cited throughout, but in no way guarantees its accuracy or completeness. The primary goal in converting retirement assets into a Roth IRA is to reduce the future tax liability on the distributions you take in retirement, or on the distributions of your beneficiaries. The information provided is to help you determine whether or not a Roth IRA conversion may be appropriate for your particular circumstances. Please review your retirement savings, tax, and legacy planning strategies with your legal/tax adviser to be sure a Roth IRA conversion fits into your planning strategies. All Rights Reserved.

Copyright © 2023 by Magellan Financial and Cory Zafke & Taylor Sundeen. All rights reserved. No part of this publication may be reproduced, distributed, or transmitted in any form or by any means, electronic or mechanical, including photocopying, recording, or by any information storage and retrieval system, without written permission of the publisher, except in the case of brief quotations embodied in critical reviews and certain other noncommercial uses permitted by copyright law.

Printed in the United States of America
First Printing, 2023
Cover and interior design by the Magellan Creative Team.

# CONTENTS

Introduction ................................................................... vii
    It Is Up To You ........................................................ vi
    Creating a ClearPath to Retirement ........................... ix

Chapter One ................................................................. 1
SOMEDAY IS NOW
What Financial Phase Are You In? ................................ 3
    Accumulation Phase ................................................. 4
    Preservation & Distribution Phase ............................. 5
Market Investments ..................................................... 7
Bank Products ............................................................. 9
Insurance Vehicles ..................................................... 11
    Immediate Annuity ................................................. 12
    Fixed Annuity ........................................................ 13
    Indexed Annuity .................................................... 14
Are Your Current Allocations Supporting Your Goals? .... 16

Chapter Two ............................................................... 19
RISK IN RETIREMENT
Risk #1: Taxes ........................................................... 21
Risk #2: Longevity Risk .............................................. 23
Risk #3: Death of a Spouse ........................................ 24
Risk #4: Market Risk .................................................. 26
Risk #5: Inflation ....................................................... 27
Risk In Retirement ..................................................... 29

## Chapter Three .................................................................31
**INCOME PLANNING**

Step #1: Develop a Vision ...............................................35
Step #2: Create a Spending Plan ....................................36
Step #3: Identify the Income Gap ...................................40
Step #4: Work with a Fiduciary .......................................41
How Do You Want to Retire? ..........................................44

## Chapter Four ...................................................................47
**SOCIAL SECURITY**

Facts About Social Security ............................................49
   Who Is Eligible? .........................................................49
   What Is Social Security? ............................................50
   When Should I File? ..................................................52
   How Much Will I Get? .................................................54
Working While Claiming Social Security ........................56
Are You Entitled to Survivor Benefits? ...........................57
   Divorce Benefits .........................................................58
Optimize Your Social Security Benefit. ..........................60

## Chapter Five ....................................................................63
**TAXES IN RETIREMENT**

Tax Me Now, Tax Me Later, Tax Me Some, Tax Me Never ......66
   Taxable ........................................................................66
   Tax-Deferred ...............................................................67
   Tax-Advantaged and Tax-Free ...................................68
How Your Social Security Benefit Is Taxed ...................70
   Provisional Income Formula ......................................71
   Income Thresholds .....................................................72
Get a Withdrawal Strategy ..............................................73
Get A Tax-Efficient Withdrawal Strategy ........................75

**Chapter Six ........................................................................ 77**
ROTH IRA CONVERSIONS: WHEN DOES IT MAKE SENSE?
The Window of Tax Opportunity................................................78
The Who, When, and What of the RMD .................................80
How to Get Rid of Your RMD ....................................................86
Diversify Your Tax Landscape. ...............................................89

**Chapter Seven.................................................................. 91**
FINAL THOUGHTS
Create a ClearPath to Retirement....................................93
Work with an Independent Professional............................94

**About the Authors........................................................... 99**
Cory Zafke...................................................................................99
Taylor Sundeen....................................................................... 100

**Glossary of Terms ........................................................ 103**

# Introduction

How much money do you need to retire? Three hundred thousand dollars? Five hundred thousand? A million? If you can just reach that number, if you get the right amount in your account, *then* you can retire. Right?

But here's the problem: no one knows how much money they need.

Every year of your life is unique and has different financial variables. **Inflation** and interest rates fluctuate. Tax brackets and rates change. Your expenses are different from year to year. You might want to help pay for a grandchild's college tuition or need to unexpectedly replace your roof. You don't know how big that pile of money needs to be to cover everything that could happen. There is no magic number that equates to financial security. If there was, planning and preparing for retirement would be simple.

Instead of chasing an imaginary number, trying to get a pile of money that is big enough to protect you from the economic challenges of the world, you can find a clear path to your retirement that relies on planning and strategy *as well as* money. Money can't solve all of your problems but using it wisely can set you up for a successful retirement.

At ClearPath Wealth Advisors, we approach retirement planning with three main principles:

- Helping you see a bigger version of what is possible in retirement.
- Helping you have fun along the way.
- Eliminating obstacles and creating efficiencies so you can see a clear path forward for your retirement goals.

### It Is Up To You

Retirement is about being able to afford your lifestyle and meet your needs without earning a paycheck. Some of the money you need will likely come from a Social Security benefit check, but the rest is up to you.

*Wait a minute, you just said it isn't about how much money you have.*

You're right, we did say that, and here's what we mean: a pile of money is not a plan. It is just a resource. A successful retirement takes careful planning and strategizing so you know when and how to use your money in the most efficient and long-lasting way. To afford your lifestyle and meet your needs, you don't need a pile of money—you need a *reliable income*. Leveraging the money that you have saved and invested and turning it into income is how you achieve your retirement goals.

Okay, that sounds straightforward enough. The catch is that it is *up to you* to figure out how to do it. The math might seem simple at first. You can just take a look at your annual budget and find the average monthly amount you spend. That's roughly what you'll need. *This year.* Maybe next year. But what if inflation goes up more than expected the following year? What if you have to withdraw more than you need to meet your **required minimum distributions** (RMDs), and your tax bracket goes up, raising your tax bill?

What if the market takes a hit and withdrawing money from your portfolio compounds your loss?

Things start to get complicated as you go down the road. That is why we named our business ClearPath Wealth Advisors. We want to help people find and make a clear path forward—not just for the next couple of years, but for the duration of their retirement. The good news is that we have seen time and again how a successful retirement depends a lot less on how much money you have in your pile and a lot more on how you leverage and protect it.

The onus is on you to figure it out. But that doesn't mean you have to do it alone. Building your retirement is a lot like building a house. You need a foundation, walls, a roof, plumbing, and electricity. But you don't need to pour the concrete and hammer the two-by-fours yourself. You hire a contractor and a set of experienced craftspeople who know what they are doing. Creating a retirement is much the same—you can hire someone you trust to make sure your foundation is secure, your walls are straight, and your roof is weatherproof. Your job is to hire good people, use your money wisely, and have fun along the way.

## Creating a ClearPath to Retirement

There is a lot of uncertainty in our economy right now. Market **volatility** is the new norm. Bonds aren't offsetting stocks like they once did. It is hard to know if you are going to run out of money or if you'll make it through safely. The name of our firm reflects our goal: we want to help you make a clear path forward for your retirement goals so you can see how this is going to work. We don't want you to just hope things will work out, watching your pile of money get smaller and crossing your fingers that it will last. We plan it out, we anticipate challenges, and we define the route, so you know what your money is doing and how it is helping you fund your retirement lifestyle.

The following chapters walk you through our process and our philosophy. We focus on living responsibly, giving each of your dollars a purpose and a goal to work toward, protecting and preserving your wealth so it can fund your lifestyle, and preparing for future expenses like taxes. There is a lot of information about finances in the world, and the internet puts all of it at your fingertips. You can find whatever you want to hear that confirms your opinions and biases. While that might feel good in the short term, your retirement is a long-term endeavor. You don't just need someone or something to tell you that you are right—you need to know you have a clear path to reach your retirement goals.

Your retired years are your chance to do more of the things you love, and to spend your time more freely. Instead of watching the market every day, trying to manage this money by yourself, and essentially taking on the workload of maintaining the financial aspects of your retirement, you can work with us to create a system. We will help you put processes in place that build efficiency into your portfolio and help solve your need for income while keeping an eye on growth for your future financial needs. Why not use our expertise and experience so you don't have to spend your retired days worrying about money?

We work with people who want to work with us—that is one of the benefits of being independent financial advisers. We aren't beholden to any particular product or service. The entire market of financial solutions is open to us, and we are available to work with anyone who agrees with our philosophy and is open to our suggestions. We apply a pragmatic approach to financial planning that doesn't forget that retirement is about having some fun, too. When we say it isn't all about the amount of money we have, we also mean that we don't want you to lose focus on the *purpose* of that money. You have worked for it, earned it, saved and invested it so that you can enjoy your golden years. Isn't it time to create a plan that takes the worry off of your plate and maximizes your enjoyment?

We want to work with good people who are happy to work with us. Give us a call at **(952) 406-8011** and start making a ClearPath to your retirement today.

Sincerely,<br>
Cory Zafke and Taylor Sundeen

# Chapter One

## SOMEDAY IS NOW

*"Setting goals is the first step in turning the invisible into the visible."*

~ Tony Robbins

Retirement is something new. It brings a new schedule, a new lifestyle, and a new perspective on life. New things are a result of change—and in retirement, a lot of things change, especially when it comes to your finances. Chances are that you haven't had a career as a financial and retirement planning expert. But once you leave your job and stop earning a paycheck, the onus is on you to organize and leverage your savings and investments to provide you with retirement income to fund your lifestyle. It is up to you to figure it out, even though you have never done it before, and you really only have one chance to get it right.

It can feel like a lot of pressure. The good news is that there are plenty of resources and helpful people who can guide you along the way and help you make informed decisions. You just need to sort through all the nonsense and noise to find them. This may come as a surprise, but not everyone in the financial industry will have *your* best interest at heart. All joking aside, it can be hard to find someone to work with who you really trust and who is focused on educating you instead of just selling you financial products and services.

New research conducted by the FINRA Investor Education Foundation and the Global Financial Literacy Excellence Center (GFLEC) at the George Washington University School of Business finds that the average saver has "alarmingly low" levels of financial knowledge.[1] The result? Low confidence when making investing decisions.

This matters because as you get closer to the time of retirement, your financial goals begin to change. Asset allocation, **risk** tolerances, and financial needs all undergo a shift, and you need to know how to respond intelligently. For many people, that means they need to get more involved in their finances. Instead of earning, saving, and investing, it is time to preserve, protect, and distribute your money. When you were working and earning, it was less important to know exactly where your money was and what it was doing. Dollar-cost averaging was on your side. In retirement, the opposite is true. Every dollar needs a job so it can achieve a specific goal. It is time to understand what you own, where it is, why it is there, and how it is serving your retirement goals.

We also want you to enjoy your retirement. Money is a resource that helps make things happen. So, we ask all our clients how they are going to use their money. We want to know their goals. Once we know what they want out of their retirement, we can work backwards to create

---

[1] Williams, Angelita, and Rote, Mike, New Research: Many U.S. Investors With Low Financial Literacy Levels Are Ill-Equipped to Manage Personal Finances, Especially Investments, FINRA, October 2019. https://www.finra.org/media-center/newsreleases/2019/many-us-investors-ill-equipped-manage-personal-finances-especially Accessed 11/17/2021

a plan that puts their money to work toward those goals. Remember all those things you were going to do *someday?* Someday is now, so it's time to make a plan for making those things happen.

---

**Fast Fact**: *According to a report by FINRA, investor knowledge in the United States is low.*[2]

---

## What Financial Phase Are You In?

Have you ever wondered why advice about wealth building varies so much from one adviser to another? This can make it difficult to know who to trust or what to believe.

**One straightforward way you can wade through the noise is to identify what financial phase you're in and then choose your assets accordingly.**

Broadly speaking, every investor who saves for retirement finds themselves going through two financial phases in life. Those two phases are the **accumulation phase** and the **distribution phase.** Some advisers also take their clients through a **preservation phase,** to help them get their retirement income secured. During this financial transition, you go from earning a paycheck to being your own paycheck. In short, you become independent, and with that independence comes the vulnerability and responsibility of protecting your assets. What follows is the *When, How,* and *Who* of the financial vehicles you'll use during these phases, including the kinds of professionals who can help guide you.

---

[2] Lin, Judy T, et al, Investors in the United States: The Changing Landscape, FINRA, December 2022, page 2, https://finrafoundation.org/sites/finrafoundation/files/NFCS-Investor-Report-Changing-Landscape.pdf Accessed 3/31/2023.

## Accumulation Phase

**WHEN:** Your *accumulation phase* begins the day you get your first job, and it can continue well into your 50s and beyond. During your working years, your focus is on growing and accumulating assets. If you're disciplined, or if you've had the foresight to set up automatic withdrawals, then you've probably gotten pretty good at this phase.

**HOW:** The accumulation phase benefits from long-term *passive investment strategies* such as **buy-and-hold** and dollar-cost averaging. Basically, you keep putting away the money, and over time the money grows. Whether the stock market goes up, down, or sideways, as long as you don't touch this money, your accounts have the potential to move upward, which is exactly the outcome you want.

**WHO:** For this phase, it's common to work with a fund manager provided by the HR department of your employer, especially if you have a 401(k) or retirement plan with an employer match. You might also work with a stockbroker or a broker-dealer for help with the buying and selling of investments. You may even try doing this kind of investing by yourself using online financial services. You are, after all, responsible for making the lion's share of the contributions.

---

*Fast Fact: Although they save more, women—whether married, widowed, or single—are more likely than men to run out of savings in retirement.*[3]

---

[3] Enda, Grace, and William G Gale. "How does gender equality affect women in retirement?" Brookings, July 2020. https://www.brookings.edu/essay/how-does-gender-equality-affect-women-in-retirement/ Accessed 11/17/2021.

## Preservation & Distribution Phase

**WHEN:** Your *distribution phase* begins on the day your accumulation phase ends. For most people, this happens sometime in their 60s, but some people retire earlier or later. Your focus during this phase is on protecting, preserving, and distributing—or spending—the money from out of your retirement accounts. You're no longer putting a portion of each paycheck into your savings; instead, *you are taking the money out* to spend it for retirement income. This fundamental shift changes everything you thought you knew about how to allocate this money.

**HOW:** During this phase, you are advised to make allocation selections based on *preservation first* and *growth second*. This is why some financial professionals usher their clients through a *preservation phase* once they reach age 40, or five to 10 years before they plan to retire. During the preservation phase, the portion of your savings required for retirement income is reallocated into financial instruments that better protect this money from market volatility. The visual below gives an idea of when the transitions from one phase to another might end or begin.

**WHO:** To be successful during the distribution phase requires much more finesse and forethought than the strategies used during the accumulation phase. Market risk isn't the only threat to your savings. It can also be damaged by tax inefficiencies, long-term care catastrophes, and the problem of required minimum distributions from tax-qualified accounts. For this reason, you'll want to work with an adviser who specializes in this phase.

## Your Three Financial Phases

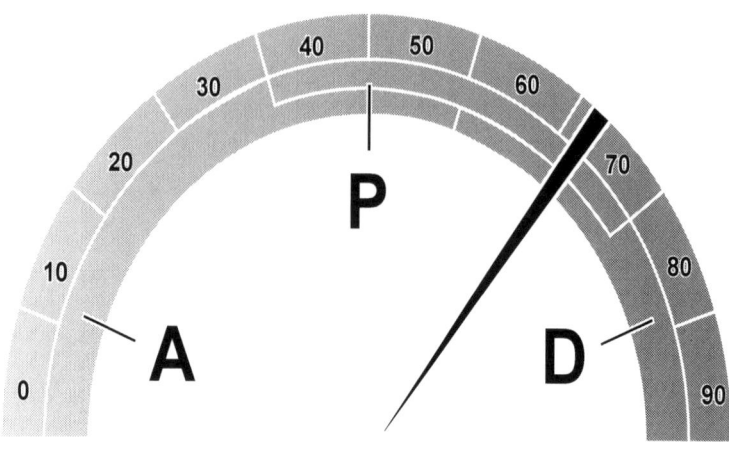

**A - Accumulation**
20s, 30s, 40s, 50s, 60s

**P - Preservation**
40s, 50s, 60s, 70s

**D - Distribution**
60s, 70s, 80s, 90+

Source: Magellan Financial

Our job, when preparing you for retirement, is to help ensure that your money lasts for the rest of your life. We do this by coordinating your allocation decisions with your retirement timeline and determining when and where you will withdraw money for income as you progress through retirement. Additionally, we want to organize your assets in a cost-efficient manner. We must take a look at the fees you are paying and determine how to reduce them as much as possible. We say you should be paying for advice, not just to be at the party. We think of the fees for many investments as cover charges at a bar or restaurant: What if you don't like the band? What if you just wanted to get a hamburger? Is the cover charge worth it?

To figure that out, we consider your sources of income, including those from a pension or Social Security, to identify how much additional income you'll need to distribute from your savings. During the distribution phase, we apply financial tools and income-creation vehicles best suited to help you transition from one phase into the next.

And now, let's talk about the financial tools you have available to help you best accomplish your goals in each phase.

*Fast Fact: About 66% of 401(k) plan assets were held inside mutual funds with the remaining in stocks, bonds, and other market investments.*[4]

## Market Investments

Market investments are one of the most recognizable assets. Virtually anyone who has an investment portfolio has some kind of market investment. This type of investing offers opportunities to profit from the future success of a business or entity. Also known as equities or securities, these positions have the potential to go up in value over time, so most people rely on some type of market investments while saving during their accumulation years. The most common market investments are stocks, bonds, mutual funds, and variable annuities.

**A stock** is an equity position in a company, named after the size of the company, small, mid, and large, organized according to the sector they do business in, such as healthcare or energy. By purchasing a share of the stock, investors can participate in the gains if the stock goes up in value. If the stock goes down in value, then people lose money.

[4] Investment Company Institute, Frequently Asked Questions: How large are 401(k)s? Independent Directors Council October 2021 https://www.ici.org/policy/retirement/plan/401k/faqs_401k. Accessed 6/27/2023.

**A bond** is a debt investment in which you are financing an activity. You loan money to an entity for a defined period of time in exchange for a fixed amount of interest. Usually thought of as the stable part of your typical portfolio, during your retirement years, bonds can expose you to risk if you need to sell early.

**Mutual funds** and exchange-traded funds (ETFs) are professionally managed pools of securities that could include both **common stocks** and bonds. Savers with similar goals combine their resources to benefit from more diversification and lower individual risk.

**Variable annuities** are a kind of annuity that offers you mutual funds inside an insurance vehicle. This gives you options for income generation and income protection, but at a cost. Please be advised that your **principal** is still not guaranteed.

The one thing all market investments have in common is that they do not guarantee the principal—or the amount you initially put into the investments. With securities, you share in both the gains and the losses with no guarantee that you will get to keep the principal or the money you earned. For the saver at or nearing retirement, this can be problematic.

While there are no protections to cover loss due to market activity, the Securities Investor Protection Corporation (SIPC) does mandate most registered broker-dealers in the U.S. This protects your accounts from the bankruptcy of the broker-dealer who serves as the custodian of your assets.

**Advantages:**
- Opportunities for market returns.
- Hedges against inflation.
- Income options available.
- Suitable for your accumulation phase.

**Disadvantages:**
- Volatility and uncertainty.
- No principal guarantees.
- Professional management fees, trade costs, and marketing fees.
- May not be suitable for someone in their distribution phase.

---

*Fast Fact:* As measured by the Consumer Price Index (CPI), the annual rate of inflation from October 2020 to October 2021 was 6.2 percent.[5]

---

## Bank Products

Unlike market investments, bank products do offer principal guarantees. The amount of money you put into the bank is guaranteed to be there when you want to take it out. Bank products are also easy to get into, with most of them costing you nothing in terms of fees or trading costs. Consumers are also able to earn an amount of interest on their money, but you're taxed on this interest, and it isn't usually high enough to keep up with inflation.

---

[5] Edelberg, Wendy, What does current inflation tell us about the future? Brookings.edu, November 2021, https://www.brookings.edu/blog/up-front/2021/11/16/what-does-current-inflation-tell-us-about-the-future/ Accessed 7/27/2023.

The most common interest-earning bank products are savings accounts, money market accounts, and certificates of deposit, known as bank CDs.

**Savings accounts** are places where you can put your money to earn a bit of interest with the ability to take it out again anytime you choose. You don't need a financial professional to get into one of these accounts, and there are no fees or trading costs involved.

**Money market accounts** work the same way—they're also interest-bearing, but they typically offer a higher rate than your regular savings account. Some money market accounts may have a minimum balance requirement, and interest rates may be tiered, meaning the more money you have in the account, the more interest you stand to earn.

**Bank CDs** are promissory notes issued by a bank. The interest rate you will earn is fixed in exchange for a period of time where you agree not to spend this money. You can choose the duration, anywhere from a few months to 10 years, with longer durations offering higher guaranteed rates.

As bank products, all funds held under this umbrella are protected by the Federal Deposit Insurance Corporation (FIDIC) for up to $250,000. This means that if the bank is robbed or the economy collapses, you're still guaranteed to get your money back. Should you choose to invest more than $250,000 with your bank, there is additional FDIC coverage available. The FDIC not only insures deposits, but it also holds the nation's financial systems accountable to certain standards, supervising their soundness and consumer protection.

**Advantages:**
- Immediate or short-term access.
- Interest rate opportunity.
- No volatility or uncertainty.
- Safety with the guarantee of principal.
- FDIC-insured.

**Disadvantages:**
- No opportunity for market gains.
- Subject to inflation risk.
- Minimum balance may be required.
- Earnings are taxed in the year they are earned.

---

*Fast Fact*: The national rate caps in November of 2021 are 0.82% for savings and money market accounts, and 0.82% to 2.17% for bank CDs.[6]

---

## Insurance Vehicles

Insurance products that fall under this umbrella might include term insurance, whole life, or universal life insurance. For this book, we're going to focus our discussion on insurance products designed for income creation.

Annuities are income-creation tools for the person at or nearing retirement. They can do what no other financial product can do: guarantee an individual's income for the rest of their life. Some income vehicles can also guarantee that income for both you and your spouse if that is what you want to do. Guarantees are backed by the financial

---

[6] FDIC, Bankers Resource Center: National Rates and Rate Caps, November 15, 2021, https://www.fdic.gov/resources/bankers/national-rates/index.html Accessed 11/17/2021.

strength of the issuing company, so you want to do your due diligence when selecting your provider.

We already talked about the type of annuity that invests in the stock market. Now, let's talk about the different annuity types that don't invest in the market investments.

## Immediate Annuity

An immediate annuity is an agreement between you and an insurance company whereby they promise to make retirement income payments to you in return for a lump sum. These payments can be set for specific durations, such as 20 years, or an unspecified period such as your lifetime, or the lifetime of you and your spouse. They can be arranged to arrive monthly, quarterly, or annually, but whichever options you choose, you will give up access to your deposit as a lump sum in exchange for access to an income.

Immediate annuities are designed to protect you against the risk of living too long. Back in the old days, if you got hit by a bus the day after committing to an annuity, the insurance company would keep the rest of your money. That did not sit well with people! Today's annuities have **beneficiary** options. This means your spouse or family members will receive any money left in the annuity even if you've been receiving income for a few years.

**Advantages:**
- Fixed interest rate.
- Safety and principal guarantees.
- Guaranteed income.
- No volatility or uncertainty.
- Protection against longevity risk.
- No **probate**.
- Simple to understand.

**Disadvantages:**
- No access to market gains.
- No access to the lump sum.
- Subject to inflation risk.

## Fixed Annuity

With a fixed annuity, you put a sum of money into the insurance agreement in exchange for an agreed-upon rate of return. These agreements are usually short-term, from one to six years, but they could be as long as 10 years. If you break the terms of the agreement and take your money out early, you may face a surrender charge. However, most fixed annuities allow you to withdraw up to 10 percent of your money annually without penalty.

Be advised that federal withdrawal rules may apply if you fund your annuity with your retirement savings. Most retirement accounts will assess a 10 percent penalty if you withdraw this money before age 59½. There are many exceptions, including early retirement, so ask your adviser about the tax implications that might be involved. Fixed annuities do grow tax-deferred. You do not have to report the interest earned or pay taxes on the growth until you go to spend the money.

**Advantages:**
- Fixed interest rate.
- Safety and principal guarantees.
- No volatility or uncertainty.
- Interest accumulates tax-deferred.

**Disadvantages:**
- No access to market gains.
- Limited **liquidity**.
- Subject to inflation risk.

### Indexed Annuity

The indexed annuity is sometimes described as a combination of the variable and the fixed annuity. It can give you a place to accumulate money for retirement while also preserving your income.

While the exact functions and retirement income guarantees of the indexed annuity can vary from one insurance company to another, what they give you are two things:

- The fixed principal guarantees
- The potential for market-linked returns.

First, you'll receive a principal guarantee backed by the issuing company. The amount of money you roll over into this vehicle is guaranteed not to go down due to stock market loss. This can be a valuable benefit for someone nearing retirement who needs this money for income.

And second, you have the opportunity to hedge against inflation via market-linked returns. The indexing system allows you to track a market index without putting your money directly into the market. These interest credits are locked in annually and they accumulate tax-deferred. Most indexed annuities also have caps, or upper limits, on how much interest you can earn. While you may not see double-digit returns, you will also not earn anything less than 0 percent.

**Indexed annuities do not credit you with a negative return, so even if the market falls, your account balance stays level.**

Indexed annuities have no fees unless you elect to purchase a rider, and most of them allow you to access your money without penalty should you have a long-term care event. The downside is that indexed annuities are typically long-term agreements of seven to 10 years. While you may access up to 10 percent of your money annually, you could also be assessed a surrender charge should you go over that amount during the contract time.

**Advantages:**
- Fixed interest rate.
- Safety and principal guarantees.
- Access to market-linked interest.
- Tax-deferred growth.
- Guaranteed income.[7]
- No loss due to market volatility.
- Hedge against inflation.
- Access to funds during a long-term care event.

**Disadvantages:**
- Limited access to funds unless there is a long-term care event.
- Longer investment timeline.

---

***Fast Fact:*** *Adding an annuity to a retirement portfolio allows you to get the same or higher income with a lower risk of outliving savings than an investments-only approach.*[8]

---

[7] Guarantees are backed by the claims-paying ability of the issuing company.

[8] Finke, Michael, and Pfau, Wade, New research from Principal shows annuities improve retirement outcomes, Principal National Life, April 2019 https://www.principal.com/about-us/news-room/news-releases/new-research-principal-shows-annuities-improve-retirement-outcomes Accessed 11/17/2021.

## The ClearPath:

In a rising market, people often neglect to think ahead and protect their assets. But when the market takes a downturn, panic can set in, and that's when people look for help and advice. Suddenly, when they see their account balances diminishing, they realize how important it is to protect and preserve the money they have spent decades earning and saving. **You don't have to wait until you are in a panic situation.** Protect your money before the market hurts you and prepare for the transition from your accumulation phase to your distribution phase so it can be as smooth as possible.

### Are Your Current Allocations Supporting Your Goals?

- Make a list of your investments and accounts.
- Identify whether they are in the market, in the bank, or under the insurance umbrella.
- Identify your financial phase and how far or near you are to needing this money for retirement.

# Chapter Two

## RISK IN RETIREMENT

*"Before anything else, preparation is the key to success."*

~ Alexander Graham Bell

A 401(k) is not a retirement plan.

This might come as a shock to some of you. A 401(k) is an account. It is most likely an account full of mutual funds, which primarily hold equities like stocks. In other words, chances are that most of the money in your 401(k) is invested in the stock market. It is important to note that we don't think any asset class or investment is inherently good or bad. There are things that work for certain situations and things that don't. When it comes to retirement, having all or most of your eggs in one basket can be risky.

So, take a look at the account balance in your 401(k) with a clear eye, knowing that most or all of it is subject to market risk. What would your balance be if the market lost 10 percent next week? 20 percent? 37 percent?

In our experience, we have found that people don't like to acknowledge that they are taking on risk. And we understand that. All of the money you have worked so long to save and grow is full of emotions and hopes, and facing the fact that you could lose a good chunk of it is an uncomfortable feeling. But a solid retirement plan has to acknowledge the risk in your portfolio so that you can make the proper adjustments. Once you retire, ups and downs in the market aren't just percentages and figures on paper anymore—they are *real* dollars that you need for income. We aren't saying all risk is bad or that you can't be in the market. We are saying you need the *appropriate* amount of risk so you know your income will be secure. You can't just *hope* it works out, because hope is not a plan.

We think of risk in three different ways when we work on retirement plans.

1. First, we consider **risk tolerance**. This is a personal question specific to your comfort with risk. How much risk *feels* right to you? Some people freak out when the market goes down two percent. Other people don't mind double digit swings. Everyone is different.
2. The second consideration is **risk capability**. This answers the question: how much can you actually afford to lose and still have enough to fund your retirement income for the rest of your life?
3. Thirdly, we consider **risk necessity**. Not all risk is bad. In fact, very often an amount of risk is necessary to keep give a portfolio the longevity it needs to keep producing income. Money required this month, this year, or next year for income can't handle big losses, but money you need in 10, 15, or 20 years from now will likely have a more robust risk tolerance and could

benefit from the potential for growth over that time period. This calculation can also help make sure you aren't taking on risk that you don't need to take.

Remember, the main goal here is to make sure you don't run out of money before you run out of life. To protect you from this threat requires careful planning. Market risk is a concern, but it isn't even close to the number one risk that retirees face today. There are a lot more threats to consider and gaining protection from them is not as simple as a one-size-fits-all solution. What follows are the big five threats to be aware of along with some strategies to address your concerns.

*Fast Fact*: Higher unemployment in 2020, offset somewhat by the continued rise in stock and house prices, increased the National Retirement Risk Index to 51%.[9]

## Risk #1: Taxes

We all know taxes exist, but many people are not aware of just how much they can affect a retirement portfolio. During your working years, you may not worry about taxes as much because many people save money in their 401(k) accounts tax deferred. That means you don't pay taxes on the money when you earn it, but when you *withdraw* it later. This keeps your annual tax bill lower and helps you accumulate a larger sum of money in your account.

---

[9] Munnell, Alicia H. et al, The National Retirement Risk Index: An Update from the 2019 SCF, Center for Retirement Research at Boston College, January 2021 https://crr.bc.edu/briefs/the-national-retirement-risk-index-an-update-from-the-2019-scf/ Accessed 1/23/2023.

But there's a catch. When you withdraw that money as income down the road, it is subject to income tax at whatever tax bracket and tax rate you are in at the time. That might not sound too alarming today, but what if taxes go up in the future? What if your RMDs bump you up into a higher tax bracket? There are several scenarios that could lead to a higher tax bill in retirement than you anticipated. The risk of diminishing your net income is a significant one; therefore, it is worth taking steps to minimize your taxes as much as possible as part of your overall retirement plan.

**Withdrawals from these accounts can increase your income, your marginal tax rate, the amount of tax you pay on your Social Security income, and the amount you pay in Medicare premiums.**

While you have zero control over tax law and what Congress does, you do have 100 percent control over what you do with this money. That is the difference between planning for vs. paying your taxes, and we will be talking more about this in the following chapters.

---

**Fast Fact**: *As of June 2021, Americans own an estimated $7.3 trillion in untaxed money in 401(k) plans.*[10]

---

[10] Investment Company Institute, Frequently Asked Questions: How large are 401(k)s? Independent Directors Council, June 2021, https://www.ici.org/faqs/faq/401k/faqs_401k Accessed 1/23/2023.

## Risk #2: Longevity Risk

We've already discussed how people are living longer, spending more time than ever before in retirement. Obviously, this stresses your portfolio. Longevity is the risk that magnifies all other risks. Your plan will get severely tested the longer you live. One area, in particular, has to do with the rising cost of healthcare and the type of services you may need later in life as your body ages.

It's long been reported that more than half of all 65-year-olds will require some form of long-term care (LTC). Long-term care refers to a wide range of services that you might need as your body ages, and these services could be performed at an assisted living center or in the comfort of your own home. Services range from simple custodial duties such as meal preparation or taking out the garbage to more intrinsic nursing services or 24-hour care.

- 48 percent of people turning age 65 will need some form of *paid* LTC services during their lifetime.[11]
- 24 percent of people turning 65 will require paid LTC for *more than two years*.[12]
- 15 percent of people turning age 65 will spend more than 2 years in a nursing home.[13]
- Men will need LTC for an average of 2.2 years.[14]
- Women will need LTC for an average of 3.7 years.[15]
- The 2021 national average for the cost of a private room in a nursing home is $108,405 annually.[16]

---

[11] Benz, Christine, 100 Must-Know Statistics About Long-Term Care: 2023 Edition, Morningstar, march 2023, https://www.morningstar.com/personal-finance/100-must-know-statistics-about-long-term-care-2023-edition Accessed 7/25/2023.

[12] Ibid.

[13] Ibid.

[14] Ibid.

[15] Ibid.

[16] Genworth, Key Cost of Care Findings, 2021, page 1, https://www.genworth.com/aging-and-you/finances/cost-of-care.html Accessed 1/23/2023.

Over the last 17 years, Genworth has seen a continuous national increase in the cost of care according to their surveys. Paying for these expenses is not only unpleasant to think about, it's a complicated problem to solve. Insurance companies have been rapidly exiting the long-term care market because of rising claims, low mortality rates, and higher prices in coverage than what most people can afford.[17] At the same time, innovative solutions are being offered using other policy options.

Because you know your health history better than anyone, this is an area where your adviser must customize a solution for you.

**Fast Fact**: *One out of every 3 seniors die from Alzheimer's or dementia, and in 2023 it cost the nation $345 billion.*[18]

## Risk #3: Death of a Spouse

This is a risk specific to married couples or anyone cohabitating with someone they love. It's a common misconception to think that after your partner dies your expenses suddenly get cut in half. Sorry, but that's not what happens. Your homeowner taxes, insurance, and mortgage expenses still need to be paid. Even if your house is paid off, the taxes and insurance do not get cut in half.

---

[17] Warshawsky, Mark J., The Second Failed Attempt At Public Insurance For Long-Term Services And Supports, Health Affairs, February 2022. https://www.healthaffairs.org/do/10.1377/forefront.20220131.939312/ Accessed 1/23/2023.

[18] Alzheimer's Association, Facts, and Figures, 2023 https://www.alz.org/alzheimers-dementia/facts-figures Accessed 3/29/2023.

**Most people in this situation find that the cost to maintain their lifestyle stays relatively the same, yet studies find that widows experience an income reduction of 35 to 40 percent upon their spouse's death.**[19]

Here's why:

When your spouse passes away, you will automatically lose at minimum one source of guaranteed **lifetime income stream** in the form of Social Security. You might also lose pension income unless that person did some planning. Losing these guaranteed checks creates a huge loss of income that somehow needs to be made up.

One solution can be to optimize your Social Security benefit. The longer you wait to file for your benefit, the larger the income benefit grows. One strategy helpful to married couples is to allow the larger of the two benefit checks to grow as big as possible. Then, when one spouse passes away, the surviving spouse is able to claim the larger of the two checks under the guidelines stipulated for survivor benefits.

---

**Fast Fact**: Studies find that widows experience an income reduction of 35% to 40% upon their spouse's death.[20]

---

[19] Every CRS Report. "Congressional Research Service report: Social Security and Vulnerable Groups—Policy Options to Aid Widows." January 2020, R46182 CRS Report, https://www.everycrsreport.com/reports/R46182.html Accessed 1/23/2023.

[20] Every CRS Report. "Congressional Research Service Report: Social Security and Vulnerable Groups—Policy Options to Aid Widows." January 2020, R46182 CRS Report, https://www.everycrsreport.com/reports/R46182.html Accessed 1/23/2023.

## Risk #4: Market Risk

Market risk is the risk of losing principal and interest due to a market correction. If that correction happens sometime during the 10 years before or after you retire, you might not have the time to make up for those losses. That could seriously compromise your portfolio's ability to generate income.

One myth commonly perpetuated by the industry is that "you can't miss the best days." A buy-and-hold strategy allows you to capture the full gains of the best days, but you also get the full losses of the worst days. Is this the best strategy to use for retirement accounts? And is this myth even true?

Let's put it to the test:

From 1980 to 2015, the average return for the S&P was 8.51 percent. If you had $100,000 in your typical buy-and-hold growth fund, and you missed the best days, you would have received an average return of 3.64 percent. If you missed the worst days, you would have earned an average return of 14.82 percent. Miss both the best and worst days, and you would have averaged a tidy 9.44 percent.[21]

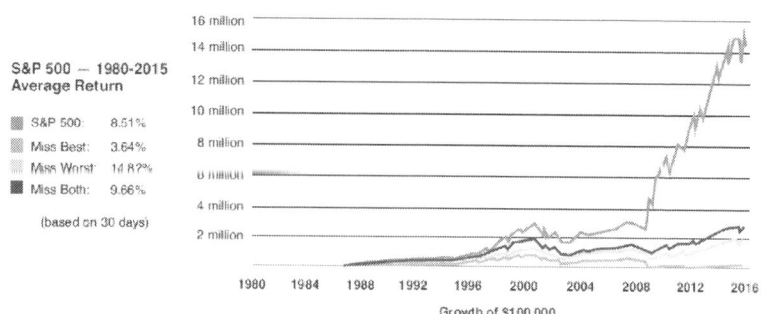

Source: Yahoo! Finance Annual Total return (%) History.

---

[21] Yahoo! Finance, SPDR S&P 500 ETF Trust (SPY) Annual total Return (%) History. https://finance.yahoo.com/quote/SPY/performance/ Accessed 1/23/2023.

If you want to remain in the market during retirement, it might be necessary to change your investment strategy. Considerations might include whether you need this money to cover all or some of your income needs and how near or far you are away from retirement.

*Fast Fact: Consumer prices were up 9.1% over the year as of June 2022, the largest increase in over 40 years.*[22]

## Risk #5: Inflation

Most people understand the basic principle of inflation: the cost of things you buy will rise. The reality of this phenomenon means that your expenses will continue to go up even after you retire. The cost of food, fuel, insurance, healthcare, professional services, etc., will increase and you will have to find a way to pay for it. Inflation is usually fairly stable, but sometimes it can spike. Case in point:

Over the 12 months ending in June 2022, the Consumer Price Index for American consumers increased 9.1 percent, the largest 12-month increase since the 12-month period ending November 1981.[23] Energy prices rose by 41.6 percent; food at home rose 12.2 percent. The price of gas? That saw a 60.2 percent increase over this same time span.[24]

---

[22] U.S. Bureau of Labor Statistics, TED: The Economics Daily, July, 2022, https://www.bls.gov/opub/ted/2022/consumer-prices-up-9-1-percent-over-the-year-ended-june-2022-largest-increase-in-40-years.htm#:~:text=Consumer%20prices%20up%209.1%20percent,U.S.%20Bureau%20of%20Labor%20Statistics&text=The%20.,gov%20means%20it's%20official. Accessed 1/23/2023.

[23] Ibid.

[24] Ibid.

The year 2013 marked the 100th anniversary of the consumer price Index—the index that measures the change in prices. To commemorate the anniversary, the Bureau of Labor Statistics revealed its cumulative data in the following chart to give you an idea of inflation's curve over a 30-year period. The line on the top represents the increase in medical care.

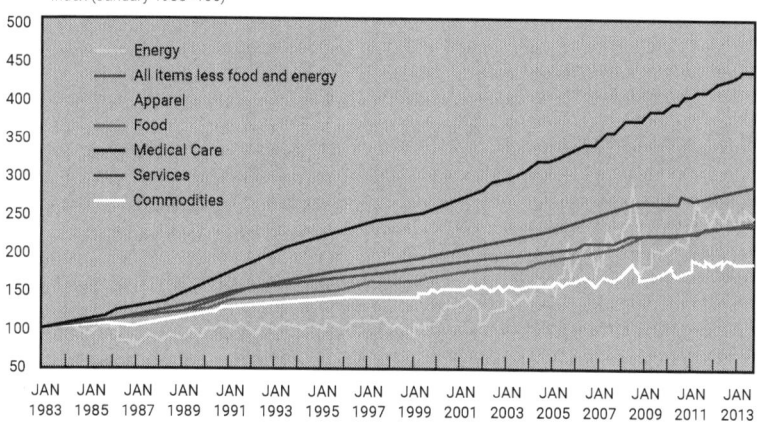

Source: U.S. Bureau of Labor Statistics.

Even when inflation rates are low, the effect is felt more by retirees, many of whom live on a fixed income. Therefore, it's not just important that you are growing your money every year during retirement; **you also want to grow your income**. Retirement income should not be stagnant. It needs to increase each year just like prices increase each year and just like your Social Security benefit increases each year based on the consumer price index. To that end, you need to make sure that the projections for growth in your retirement plan are reasonable ones. When your financial professional shows you a chart or graph of your projected income, make sure you ask what kind of return it is based on. If it is relying on an eight percent return each year, that isn't realistic.

---

**Fast Fact**: *More than 70% of individuals aged 50 and older are concerned that inflation will cause serious economic hardship during their retirement.*[25]

---

## The ClearPath:

Solving the problem of risk during retirement involves choosing the right solutions at the right time and using the right rules to your advantage. This is a moving target, however, because the financial industry is always changing and evolving. New laws, regulations, rules, interest rates, global economic events, and other variables occur all the time. What works today may not work tomorrow. While we can't know exactly what is going to happen in the future, we can plan for uncertainty and the need for increasing income over time. Take action against these risks now before the current windows of opportunity close.

### Risk In Retirement

- Make a list of your investment accounts.
- Identify whether they are invested in the stock market, bank products, or life insurance.
- Identify what risks these financial tools are helping you to address: taxes, longevity, death of a spouse, market risk, or inflation.

---

[25] Block, Sandra, Protect Your Retirement Income from Inflation, Kiplinger, September 2022 https://www.kiplinger.com/personal-finance/inflation/605175/protect-your-retirement-income-from-inflation Accessed 1/24/2023.

# Chapter Three

## INCOME PLANNING

*"A goal without a plan is just a wish."*

*~ Antoine de Saint-Exupéry*

Receiving an income without working: every retiree's dream! You have worked hard, saved, invested, and now it is time to enjoy the fruits of your labor. If you can just get to that magic number—the day your pile of money is big enough to sustain you—then you can afford to retire.

It's a nice dream, isn't it? We're here to tell you it's just that, though: a dream. The reality is that *there is no magic number, no amount of money* that will allow you to retire. This might not make sense at first. Of course, you need money to retire, but that is just *one* of the things you need. Money is a resource that you can use to create a retirement plan that will sustain you. Because you don't just need money when you are retired, you need *income*.

Not only do you need income, but you also you need an *increasing* income. Many people think their spending will stay the same or go down after they retire, but we rarely see that happen. Once you retire, every day is Saturday, and you have the time and energy to do the things you have always wanted to do.

One of the best examples of this was a woman we worked with who we will call Ginny. She was born in 1944 and took care of people her whole life. She had a long career as a nurse, and cared for her in-laws when they began suffering from dementia. She was happy to do it, but the time and energy that her career and family obligations required didn't allow Ginny to spend much time or money on herself. When she finally decided to retire, we found that she didn't require very much income to maintain her lifestyle. Ginny hadn't made any travel plans or preparations for other large expenditures because she wasn't used to thinking she could. We were happy to help set her up with the income she needed, but we encouraged her to think about spending more. She could afford it, and these were her golden years, after all.

At first, Ginny didn't like the idea of spending more. She was accustomed to seeing her account balances and enjoyed the feeling of security that having this money gave her. When we showed her how to structure her money for income instead of account balance amounts, however, the lightbulb went on in her head. She couldn't believe she could visit her grandkids in Colorado twice a year, go out to eat every weekend, and take a cruise in the winter. Thinking about income changed Ginny's retirement and her lifestyle for the better.[26]

You've been told during your working years that your expenses will decline once you enter into retirement. No more commuting, or paying for things like dry cleaning and childcare. Your mortgage will be paid off, the need to save

---

[26] The above story is a fictional story using actual figures from sources believed to be reliable. This example is shown for illustrative purposes only. Estimated projections do not represent or guarantee the actual results of any transaction, and no representation is made that any transaction will, or is likely to, achieve results similar to those shown.

for retirement will be gone. Plus Social Security is a tax-advantaged source of income.

But—and this is where people start losing sleep—the reality for today's retirees looks quite a bit different. Most people are retiring with some amount of debt, a second mortgage, and kids who are in college. Social Security only replaces about 40 percent of the average worker's pre-retirement income, and experts suggest you will need 70 to 85 percent or more of pre-retirement earnings to live comfortably.[27] Where is the rest of the income going to come from?

For most, the answer has to do with tax-deferred accounts like the 401(k). But what is a 401(k)? It's not a pension, it's not a paycheck, it's not even a guarantee. It's a collection of investments vulnerable to stock market volatility. Furthermore, none of the taxes on this money have ever been paid. Every time you go to spend this money, some amount of taxes must be paid. So, how do you take this collection of investments and turn them into a steady, reliable income that can support you and the people you care about without running out?

This is a question that needs to be answered before you head into golden years, and for today's retirees, that question has to be answered by none other than YOU.

---

**Fast Fact**: *More than half of American workers—56%—are worried that they won't be able to achieve a financially secure retirement.[28]*

---

[27] Benz, Christine, Forget Income Replacement, Focus on Supplying Cash Flow Needs, Morningstar, August 2021, https://www.morningstar.com/articles/808839/forget-income-replacement-focus-on-supplying-cash-flow-needs Accessed 2/21/2023.

[28] Bond, Tyler, Doonan, Dan, and Kennealy, Kelly, Retirement Insecurity 2021, The National Institute on Retirement Security, Feb 2021, https://www.nirsonline.org/wp-content/uploads/2021/02/FINAL-Retirement-Insecurity-2021-.pdf Accessed 2/21/2023.

Let's take a close look at the way things used to be from an income standpoint. Back in the 1980s when you retired, you got a pension replacing around 50 percent or more of your paycheck, plus an amount from Social Security that was also guaranteed. If you had any money in your savings or checking account, that was like icing on the cake. Bank CDs in the 1980s were paying out double-digit returns, so not only were you earning interest from your savings, but your income arrived without you having to invest in the stock market or expose any of your money to risk.

Today, most people aren't retiring with pensions. The percentage of workers retiring with a pension has shrunk from 60 percent in the early 1980s to only 7 percent in 2021.[29] Now, we have programs like the 401(k) where people save. When it's time to retire, you're in charge of taking your savings and turning it into a regular, reoccurring paycheck. But as market investments, none of this money is guaranteed. So, you'll want to develop an income plan that examines how your withdrawals will be taxed, both now and in the future, and how your income will be protected from both long-term and short-term losses. In this way, you'll be able to retire with peace of mind and the freedom to pursue all the activities you always dreamed you'd be doing once you retired.

What follows is a four-step process to help you turn those investments into the amount of income that you deserve.

---

[29] Worker Participation in Employer-Sponsored Pensions: Data in Brief, Congressional Research Service, November 2021, https://sgp.fas.org/crs/misc/R43439.pdf Accessed 2/21/2023.

*Fast Fact*: Studies consistently show that friendships are as important as family ties in predicting psychological well-being in adulthood and old age.[30]

## Step #1: Develop A Vision

Television commercials, brochures, and promotional materials about investment products and retirement tools all have photos of people enjoying retirement. Walking along a beach or having dinner with friends are common scenes. But this is real life, not made-for-TV retirement. So ask yourself, what do you want your retirement to look like?

Do you want to travel less or travel more? Downsize or maintain your current lifestyle? Spend all your money, live on the interest, or preserve a specific amount for a legacy?

Your retirement vision should be based on you, your family, and the things that you like to do, not someone else's definition of what the ideal retirement should look like. Not everyone wants to buzz around the country in an RV.

- When you close your eyes and picture yourself retired, where are you?
- Who are you with?
- What are you doing?
- How will you spend your mornings?
- Your afternoons?
- What does your ideal evening look like?

---

[30] Ng, Yee To; Huo, Meng; Gleason, Marci; Neff, Lisa; Charles, Susan; Fingerman, Karen, Friendships in Old Age: Daily Encounters and Emotional Well-Being, Journals of Gerontology Series B, March 2021, https://www.ncbi.nlm.nih.gov/pmc/articles/PMC7887723/ Accessed 2/21/2023.

Studies find that living a meaningful life with a sense of purpose is fundamental to your well-being during retirement, and strong personal relationships and broader social engagement lead to better physical health.[31]

After spending a lifetime developing an identity that is focused on career and means of income, retiring without developing a vision can be a shock to the system. It's never too late to identify the kinds of activities that give you a sense of worthwhile fulfillment and the people with whom you want to be spending more time.

---

*Fast Fact*: Plan on approximately 15% of your retirement expenses to be related to health care; the more health issues you expect, the higher the income replacement rate you'll want to work into your plan.[32]

---

## Step #2: Create A Spending Plan

Retirement income is the first substantive thing we talk about with people. Once you have a vision or a goal for your retirement, the real work of finding a way to fund it begins. To create an accurate spending plan, we need to gather information about when you want to retire, how you plan to spend your time, what your Social Security benefit will be, and what other guaranteed sources of income you might have in addition to that benefit. It is time to figure out how much money you spend every month currently,

---

[31] Benefits of Social Connections for Seniors, A Senior Living Resource, October 2022, https://www.whereyoulivematters.org/social-connections-and-senior-living/ Accessed 2/21/2023.

[32] Fidelity Viewpoints, How Much Will You Spend in Retirement? Fidelity, September 2021, https://www.fidelity.com/viewpoints/retirement/spending-in-retirement Accessed 2/21/2023.

and how much you will spend in the future. The more information we have, the more efficiently we can structure your retirement income plan.

**The big secret in retirement has little do with how much money you have, and much more to do with how you spend your money and where you spend it from.**

Understanding how to use your money—and *when* to use which money from which account—is the mark of good income planning. All dollars are not created equal. Some are taxed as income. Some are not. Some affect the taxation of your Social Security benefit. Some don't. There are many things to consider before you just withdraw cash to pay your bills.

The way we approach how to spend your money is by examining withdrawal order. Which money should you spend first? Non-taxable money in your **Roth IRA**? Should you take IRA money first to reduce future RMDs? There are a lot of moving parts to an income plan. We believe withdrawal order, for the most part, should look like this:

1. Dip into your non-qualified money first. That includes equities, mutual funds, some annuities, etc. Only the gains are taxable on this money, so you can get more bang for your buck, so to speak. When you withdrawal non-qualified money, you pay fewer taxes than you would from your qualified accounts
2. Next comes qualified money like IRAs, 401(k)s, 403(b)s, etc. This money hasn't been taxed as income yet and won't be until you withdraw it.
3. Lastly, we look to your Roth accounts. Whatever is left of this non-taxable money when you pass away will also be tax-free for 10 years for your beneficiaries.

While spending in retirement will look different for everybody, there is a simple way to figure this out for yourself. Developing a spending plan to understand what you're spending now is key to identifying the things that are essential to achieving your retirement vision.

This step includes digging deeper into your expenses by asking yourself which expenses are a *want* and which are a *need*? We will be defining these terms because the first 10 years of retirement are generally when you're going to feel the best, do the most, and possibly spend the most. So, we want to make sure you have what you *need* to be able to do what you *want*.

Architects draft blueprints, pilots create flight plans, and writers develop book outlines. Financial advisers design spending plans.

Ideally, you want to track your spending for three to four months. Your spending categories—such as travel, fuel, groceries, clothing—can be broken down into two broader groupings: Needs and Wants.

Needs include the things required by the body for basic survival. They are also called **non-discretionary expenses**.

- Food
- Water
- Shelter
- Utilities
- Insurance
- Clothing
- Healthcare
- Medicine/prescriptions
- Transportation

Wants might be essential to the mind and spirit, but they are things the body could live without. They are also called **discretionary expenses.**

- Travel
- Vacations
- Hobbies
- Charitable donations
- Grandchildren spoiling
- New cars
- Dining out
- RV expenses

To develop a spending plan, look at what you are currently spending every month in the six areas of housing, healthcare, transportation, personal insurance, food, and miscellaneous expenses. Here is a breakdown of these six areas to give you an idea of what kinds of things you should include in each category.

**Housing**: includes mortgage cost, property taxes, homeowner's insurance, rent, utilities, repairs, maintenance, plus other fees and expenses.

**Healthcare**: includes medical services, medications, and supplies, plus health insurance.

**Transportation**: includes vehicle maintenance, fuel, auto insurance, public transportation, and rideshare expenses.

**Personal Insurance**: includes life insurance, umbrella policies, disability insurance, long-term care, final expenses, or any other insurance.

**Food**: includes both groceries and dining out.

**Miscellaneous**: includes outstanding loan payments, credit card payments, entertainment, travel and vacation, hobbies, gifts, education expenses, charitable donations, and any other expenses not listed.

*Fast Fact*: Most people can assume a retirement income replacement ratio of 80%, meaning they'll spend about 80% of the income they were making before retirement.[33]

As you start to record all the amounts in these six areas, you might find yourself thinking about how some of these expenses will change once you are retired. You might also realize that an item you thought was a *want* is really a *need*, meaning your retirement won't feel satisfying or meaningful without it. A true plan allows for flexibility and gives a way to finance both *needs* and *wants*.

## Step #3: Identify the Income Gap

The **income gap** is the difference between your retirement living expenses and the income from guaranteed sources such as pensions or Social Security. You might also have other sources of guaranteed income such as rental income or payment from an annuity.

Living expenses - guaranteed income = the income gap

Breaking down the income into two different types will help inform your decisions for funding the income gap.

**To fund your income needs**, consider using long-term, guaranteed sources of income that are not in the stock market such as annuities. This strategy will give you a sure thing. Even if a pandemic breaks out during the year that you retire and the market takes a 30 percent nosedive, the expenses you need to survive will still be covered.

---

[33] Fidelity Viewpoints, "How Much Will You Spend in Retirement?" Fidelity, September 2021 https://www.fidelity.com/viewpoints/retirement/spending-in-retirement Accessed 2/21/2023.

**To fund your income wants** and outplace the long-term effects of inflation, consider using a combination of market investments such as stocks, mutual funds, exchange-traded funds, or managed money. This strategy will give you a maybe. During times of market turmoil, as long as your basic expenses are met, you should be able to leave these investments alone as part of your long-term growth strategy. When the market is up or the time is opportune, you may cash in these investments to fund one of your retirement dreams.

---

*Fast Fact*: Only 23% of Americans have a comprehensive written plan for retirement.[34]

---

Gordon and Stella are wondering if they have enough money saved to retire. They know that their bills total $8,070 a month for an annual expense of $96,840. When they sit down and look closer at their needs vs. wants, they get a clearer picture: their basic needs can be met with only $60,000 a year.

"But that doesn't include our trip to Australia," Stella notices.

"No, it does not," says their adviser. "So that's what we must identify. How much of the $8,000 a month do you want to have as a sure thing, and how much are you comfortable with as a maybe?"

To answer that question, the adviser takes them through the income gap exercise. They discover that they will receive a total income of $32,000 from Social Security and

---

[34] Deaton, Holly, Most Americans Have No Financial Plan. The Ones Who Do Praise the Benefits, RIA Intel, May 2022, https://www.riaintel.com/article/2aucrzsa72lr93ymbe7eo/wealth-management/most-americans-have-no-financial-plan-the-ones-who-do-praise-the-benefits Accessed 2/21/2023.

another $25,000 annually from Gordon's pension. This gave them a total of $57,000 in guaranteed retirement income.

They have no other sources of guaranteed income.

Doing the math, Gordon and Stella calculated an income gap of $3,000 a year for their needs and a gap of $36,840 for their wants. This gave them a total gap of $39,840 annually.

"So, how much of this income gap do you want to fund as a sure thing and how much do you want to fund as a maybe?"

"Well, if we're talking about our trip to Australia," says Stella, "I won't feel like I'm living my dream retirement without it. So, I need that trip to be a sure thing."

Traveling to Australia for Stella was not a maybe. She needed to know that it would be a sure thing.

By getting clear about both their retirement vision and their spending, Gordon and Stella are now able to choose their investments accordingly.

## Step #4: Work With A Fiduciary

No adviser wants to look at someone and tell them that they can't afford to retire, yet that's why people seek counsel. It is an adviser's job to help steer their clients right, and sometimes that means telling someone what they *need* to hear rather than what they *want* to hear. But sometimes advisers experience what we in the industry call a *conflict of interest*.

The key thing to realize is that financial professionals go by many different names, and not all of them are held to the same standards of care. Sometimes because of where they work, an adviser will have an inherent conflict of interest when it comes to giving you advice. If they tell you, for example, that you're going to run out of money the way things currently stand, then you might make a change to your portfolio, which affects their commission and causes *them* to lose money.

For this reason, you always want to work with **a fiduciary** professional.

---

**Fast Fact**: *A fiduciary duty comprises of a duty of care, **trust**, and loyalty that requires an adviser to serve in the best interest of the client at all times.*[35]

---

Under a fiduciary duty of loyalty, an investment adviser must eliminate or disclose of conflicts of interest which might cause the adviser—consciously or unconsciously—to give advice that is not in the best interest of you, the client. A fiduciary is also required to base their advice *not* on commission fees or the flavor of the day but on the client's objectives.

This is why fiduciaries begin *not* with the numbers but with a series of questions designed *to get to know you*. Generally speaking, fiduciaries are more concerned with getting to know the person and establishing a relationship of trust rather than selling you a certain product or investment.

---

[35] Securities and Exchange Commission, Commission Interpretation Regarding Standard of Conduct for Investment Advisers, July 2019. https://www.sec.gov/rules/interp/2019/ia-5248.pdf Accessed 2/21/2023.

## The ClearPath:

Retirement is all about income. There is no amount of money to save that will unlock a successful retirement, but there is an amount of *income* that can help you achieve your retirement goals. Leveraging your assets and organizing them in an efficient withdrawal order will help you maximize your income, minimize your tax liability, and help keep more of your money in your pocket for your lifestyle expenses. Best of all, by creating a secure income plan, you will know how much money you can rely on each month regardless of what happens in the market.

### How Do You Want to Retire?

- Figure out what you want your retirement to look like.
- Develop a spending plan.
- Identify your income gap.
- Work with a fiduciary who puts your best interests above their own.

# Chapter Four

## SOCIAL SECURITY

*"Get the fundamentals down and the level of everything you do will rise."*

~ Michael Jordan

Social Security is a slam dunk, right? You decide when you want to stop working and then you file to get your monthly benefits. Bada bing, bada boom. That might be when you're 62 years old, or 70 years old, or anywhere between. There is a penalty for filing before your **full retirement age** (FRA), however, and your benefit goes up every year you wait to file until age 70. And did you know that a portion of your Social Security income could be taxed depending on your adjusted gross income?

Okay, we've made our point—filing for Social Security is more complicated that many people think it is. There are a lot of balls in the air when you retire, and your Social Security benefit is one of them. It doesn't operate in a vacuum. You need to know how it affects the other parts of your retirement plan, and how those parts affect your Social Security benefit.

When should you file for Social Security? The honest answer is that we don't know. A lot of people file for Social Security and then figure out the rest of their income needs. But we know that if you turn that Social Security income stream on too early, it could create problems down the road. You might not end up having enough income later, or it might bump you into a higher tax bracket that ends up diminishing your overall net income. We don't know when you should file until we take a look at your entire financial picture and retirement goals.

By creating a plan that considers your Social Security benefit options along with all the other financial variables in your portfolio, we hope to not just get you the biggest benefit check, but the most overall net income. That means we do the calculus of how taxes, tax brackets, potential future growth opportunities, inflationary pressure, and other variables affect your financial future.

This chapter is dedicated to giving you clarity around Social Security benefits. Social Security is a rare source of guaranteed income, and you should get the most out of it. It will likely be a significant source of your retirement income: 30 percent or more of retirement income for most older recipients comes from Social Security benefits.[36] This is an earned benefit most people have paid into their entire working life. So how do you get the most out of it? Can you receive benefits even if you've never held a job? What happens if your spouse passes away? Can you work and collect Social Security at the same time?

This chapter is here to give you some answers.

---

[36] Social Security Administration Fact Sheet June 2023 https://www.ssa.gov/news/press/factsheets/basicfact-alt.pdf Accessed 7/20/2023.

> *Fast Fact*: Just over half—53%—of near retirees earned a D or lower on a quiz testing their knowledge about basic Social Security rules.[37]

## FACTS ABOUT SOCIAL SECURITY: Who, What, When, and How

Ninety-seven percent of older Americans receive Social Security as part of their retirement plan.[38] Known in its official capacity as *the retired worker benefit*, this is a lifetime benefit that pays out to a single individual every month for as long as that person lives.

### WHO Is Eligible?

Anyone who works and pays Social Security taxes may become eligible for benefits by earning credits. The number of quarterly work credits required to receive retirement benefits depends on when you were born.

- If you were born in 1929 or later, you need 40 qualifying credits (QC) or 10 years of "substantial earnings".
- Work credits earned remain on your Social Security record.
- Benefit payments are based on the top 35 working years, adjusted for inflation using the Average Wage Index (AWI).
- If you stop working, then return to work later, you can add more credits to qualify.
- You can't receive retirement benefits on your record until you have completed the required number of credits.

---

[37] Franklin, Mary Beth, Third of near-retirees fail basic Social Security quiz, Investment News, April 2021 https://www.investmentnews.com/third-of-near-retirees-fail-basic-social-security-quiz-204852 Accessed 12/19/2022.

[38] Center on Budget and Policy Priorities, Policy Basics: Top Ten Facts about Social Security, updated March 2022, https://www.cbpp.org/research/social-security/top-ten-facts-about-social-security Accessed 1/11/2022.

There is another way you can qualify for benefits even if you have not earned your 40 credits. Married individuals who never worked or have low earnings can get up to half of their spouse's benefit amount. There are also other benefits for family members of a retired worker, subject to a family maximum.
- Spouses aged 62 or older may get spousal benefits.
- Spouses younger than age 62 may get benefits if they are taking care of a child younger than age 16 or disabled.
- Former spouses if they are age 62 or older may get divorce benefits, even if the former spouse has remarried, as long as they do not remarry.
- Widows and widowers may get survivor benefits as long as they haven't remarried before age 60 (age 50 if disabled).
- Disabled children, even if they are age 18 or older, may get benefits.
- Children up to age 18, or up to age 19 if full-time students and not graduated from high school, may get benefits.

### WHAT Is Social Security?

Social Security is a federal insurance program that provides benefits to retired people and to those who are employed or disabled. It is a pay-as-you-go system where taxes are paid into the program by working people to provide the benefits for people who qualify for them. It's also a good deal.

**Most people born between 1940 and 1999 who reach age 65 are scheduled to receive more in lifetime benefits than they contributed in taxes.**[39]

What the system is not: Social Security is NOT a system where you pay taxes into an account with your name on it so that when you retire, you can start pulling that money out. It's also not designed to replace 100 percent of your working income. The system was designed to give the average American worker insurance against the risk of living too long.

- In 1940, the life expectancy of a 65-year-old was almost 14 years; today it is over 20 years.[40]
- In 2023, about 67 million Americans will receive over $1 trillion in Social Security benefits paid during the year.[41]
- The estimated average monthly Social Security benefit payable in December 2022 was $1,825 a month.[42]

*Fast Facts: PIA is the primary insurance amount or the amount of money you're going to receive at full retirement age. FRA is the acronym for full retirement age. SSA is the acronym for the Social Security Administration. NRA is your normal retirement age, also known as your FRA.*[43]

---

[39] Steuerle, Eugene C; Cosic, Damir; Quakenbush, Caleb, How Do Lifetime Social Security Benefits and Taxes Differ by Earnings? Urban Institute, February 2019. https://www.urban.org/research/publication/how-do-lifetime-social-security-benefits-and-taxes-differ-earnings Accessed 1/11/2023.

[40] Social Security Administration Fact Sheet, 2023, https://www.ssa.gov/news/press/factsheets/basicfact-alt.pdf Accessed 7/20/2023.

[41] Ibid.

[42] Ibid.

[43] Social Security Administration, Glossary of Social Security Terms, https://www.ssa.gov/agency/glossary/ Accessed 1/11/2023.

## WHEN Should I File?

The basics of getting an income strategy come down to a question of *now* or *later*. The longer you wait, the bigger your check will get. Once you reach full retirement age (FRA), delayed credits grow your payment at a rate of about 8 percent per year.[44] But there is a tradeoff: you won't receive a check during the years you wait.

*Now:* The earliest you can take your benefit is age 62. This is known as filing early and it comes with an "actuarial reduction" that will reduce your benefits. For example, if you turn age 62 in 2023, your benefit would be about 30 percent lower than it would be at your full retirement age (FRA).[45] Each year, month, and day you wait to file increases your starting benefit amount incrementally. Your FRA is between ages 66 or 67, depending on the year you were born, at which time you'll receive 100 percent of your earned benefits.

*Later:* The latest you can wait to file is age 70. Those delayed credits begin accumulating after FRA and they keep increasing the amount of your benefit until you reach age 70. The following visual is based on a Full Retirement Age of 66 and gives you an idea of how much you stand to gain or lose when deciding on now or later. It is also important to note that all future **Cost-of-Living-Adjustment (COLA)** increases will be based on the starting amount at your chosen filing age.

---

[44] AARP, What are delayed retirement credits and how do they work? Dec 2022, https://www.aarp.org/retirement/social-security/questions-answers/delayed-retirement-credits.html Accessed 1/16/2023.

[45] Social Security Administration, Retirement Benefits, 2023 https://www.ssa.gov/pubs/EN-05-10035.pdf Accessed 1/11/2023.

## Projected Income Benefits Based on a $2,000 Primary Insurance Amount

| AGE | BENEFIT % | BENEFIT $ |
|---|---|---|
| **Actuarial Reduction** | | |
| 62 | 70% | $1,400 |
| 63 | 75% | $1,500 |
| 64 | 80% | $1,600 |
| 65 | 86.7% | $1,734 |
| 66 | 93.3% | $1,866 |
| **Full Retirement Age (FRA)** | | |
| 67 | 100% | $2,000 |
| **Delayed Retirement Credits** | | |
| 68 | 108% | $2,160 |
| 69 | 116% | $2,320 |
| 70 | 124% | $2,480 |

Source: RetirementYou source materials.

The decision of when to file for your benefit may be informed by your personal health and relationships. Married people especially will want to look at this decision from a two-person perspective. By waiting to file, your benefit will grow, and if you're married, this could result in a much bigger benefit check for your surviving spouse. **If you file early, however, you lock in the early-filing amount for life.**

**Fast Fact**: *75% of near retirees incorrectly answered that if their spouse died, they would continue to receive both their own Social Security benefit and that of their deceased spouse. The correct answer is that the survivor receives just one check: the higher of the two benefits.*[46]

Deciding when to file for your benefit is also a financial decision that could go on to impact every other aspect of your retirement plan. There are tax consequences, income thresholds to be aware of, and ways that your **traditional IRA** income could affect the amount of taxes you pay on your Social Security income. Additionally, the employees of the Social Security administration are legally prohibited from giving filing advice. For this reason, a lot of people seek advice from advisers.

### HOW Much Will I Get?

Your primary insurance amount or PIA is Social Security lingo for the amount of money you are going to receive when you start benefit payments. It is based on four things:
- How long you worked.
- How much you made each year.
- The rate of inflation.
- The age at which you begin taking your benefit.

Because your benefits are funded by your wages, Social Security calculates an average of your 35 highest-earning years using an indexed system called the Average Wage Index (AWI) that brings your older earnings up to near-current wage levels. For example, the $14,249 salary you

---

[46] Franklin, Mary Beth, Third of near-retirees fail basic Social Security quiz, Investment News, April 2021 https://www.investmentnews.com/third-of-near-retirees-fail-basic-social-security-quiz-204852 Accessed 1/11/2023.

earned back in 1983 would be indexed by the system and converted into today's dollars for a salary valued at $65,712 for the worker retiring in 2023.[47]

Social Security also provides you with an *increasing* income to help address inflation risk. Legislation enacted in 1973 gives a cost-of-living adjustment (COLA) to your benefit. This means **your payments are designed to help keep pace with inflation.** Based on the increase in the Consumer Price Index (CPI-W), the COLA for 2018 was 2.8 percent; the highest ever COLA was 14.3 percent in 1980; the latest COLA in 2023 is for 8.7 percent.[48] Over the course of a 20-year retirement, these increases can really add up.

The more you earn during your working years, the higher your benefit will be, but there is a maximum amount of income that is taxable. This amount has changed over the years. For 2023, earnings over $160,200 may not be taxed by Social Security.[49] Because most people earn their highest salary during the later years of their working life, it's also important to know that working *while* receiving Social Security could cost you in taxes and penalties.

***Fast Fact****: Average-income single adults retiring at age 65 in 2020 will receive more than $600,000 in benefits, and married couples will receive nearly $1.2 million from Medicare and Social Security.*[50]

---

[47] Social Security Administration, Benefit Calculation Examples for Workers Retiring in 2023, Office of the Chief Actuary https://www.ssa.gov/oact/progdata/retirebenefit1.html Accessed 2/09/2023.

[48] Social Security Administration, Cost-of-Living Adjustment (COLA) Information for 2023, https://www.ssa.gov/cola/ Accessed 1/11/2023.

[49] Social Security Benefits Planner, Maximum Taxable Earnings, https://www.ssa.gov/planners/maxtax.html Accessed 1/11/2023.

[50] Steuerle, Eugene C. and Smith, Karen E., Social Security & Medicare Lifetime Benefits and Taxes: 2022, Tax Policy Institute, Feb 2023, page 5, https://www.taxpolicycenter.org/publications/social-security-medicare-lifetime-benefits-and-taxes-2022/full Accessed 7/10/2023.

## Working While Claiming Social Security

Yes, it's possible to legally collect Social Security even while you're still working, but you'll want to be aware of the rules. Social Security has what they call an *earnings test* that applies to income reported on a W2 or a 1099 form. That does not include income from pensions, retirement accounts, annuities, and investments. Any reported income earned above the earnings test amount may be penalized.

Keep in mind that any penalties that come out of your paycheck do eventually make their way back to you. The Social Security Administration will increase your benefits later, but by later, we're talking about 15 or so years. So, you might want to do some planning if you want to work while claiming, especially if you're married.

Between the ages of 62 and 66 (or full retirement age), if you are working and collecting Social Security, **every $1 of income you earn over the threshold—which for 2023 is $21,240—will cost you a 50 percent penalty**.[51] Consider either working part-time to earn less than $21,240 or waiting to file for your benefit until after you reach full retirement age.

The year you reach full retirement age, two things happen:
1. The SSA uses a different formula to assess the work penalty.
2. It raises the income threshold

**During the year you reach full retirement age, they will only deduct $1 for every $3** that you earn above the (higher) income limit, which for 2023 is $56,520.[52]

---

[51] Social Security Administration, Benefits Planner: Retirement: Getting Benefits While Working https://www.ssa.gov/planners/retire/whileworking.html Accessed 1/04/2023.
[52] Ibid.

Furthermore, they will only count the earnings you received before the month you reached full retirement age. In other words, once you reach your FRA, you can work as much as you want and still receive your Social Security benefit without penalty. However, taxes would still apply based on your total earnings and a portion of Social Security.

*Fast Fact*: *According to a SSA Office of the Inspector General report, 80% of widows and widowers eligible for survivor benefits could lose an additional $530.9 million in benefits over their lifetimes due to incorrect filing.*[53]

## Are You Entitled To Survivor Benefits?

Spousal benefits—including divorce benefits—are Social Security benefits paid out to married individuals who may qualify even if they didn't work. If you did work and are entitled to a benefit on your own work record, the Social Security Administration automatically gives you the higher of the two benefit amounts.

Spousal benefits are based on a *living* spouse or ex-spouse's work history; survivor benefits are based on a *deceased* spouse or ex-spouse's work history. Survivor benefits are a category of spousal benefits that pay out only after the death of a spouse. Also called widow or widower benefits, there are some seemingly perplexing rules about these benefits— when and how you file for them matters.

---

[53] SSA, Office of the Inspector General Audit Report Summary, Retirement Beneficiaries Potentially Eligible for Widow(er)'s Benefits, June 2020, https://oig.ssa.gov/audit-reports/2020-06-09-audits-and-investigations-audit-reports-A-13-13-23109/ Accessed 1/11/2023.

For example, you cannot file for survivor's benefits online, and you may not receive survivor benefits if you remarry before the age of 60.[54] You must also have been married for a minimum of nine months prior to the death of your spouse.

The survivor benefit is based on two things:
1. When the deceased filed.
2. When the survivor files.

When one spouse passes away, the survivor (given they meet all the requirements) has the option to receive the larger of two benefit amounts:
1. Their own benefit check.
2. The benefit check of the deceased.

For example, if your deceased spouse was receiving $3,000 a month, and you are only receiving $1,500 a month, you can apply for survivor benefits and receive the $3,000 a month check instead. **With widow/widower benefits, it's also possible to allow your own benefit check to grow,** gaining those **delayed retirement credits** while receiving a survivor benefit, and then switching over to your own benefit once you reach age 70.[55]

## Divorce Benefits

Divorce benefits might feel like survivor benefits, depending on how you felt about the marriage. The good news is you can receive divorce benefits on a living or deceased ex-spouse's work history, even if they remarry. If

---

[54] Social Security Administration, If You Are the Survivor, updated 2022, https://www.ssa.gov/benefits/survivors/ifyou.html#:~:text=If%20you%20remarry%20after%20you,1213%20to%20request%20an%20appointment Accessed 1/11/2023.
[55] Ibid.

you remarry, then spousal benefits based on your previous marriage would no longer apply.

To qualify, you must be at least 62 years old, you and your spouse must have been married for at least 10 years, and in cases where you haven't yet filed for benefits, you must have been divorced for at least two years.[56] If your ex-spouse is deceased, then you may still receive benefits as long as you don't remarry before age 60 (age 50 if disabled). Divorce benefits apply to both the ex-wife and the ex-husband, and they also apply to couples in a same-sex marriage. Your ex has no say on whether or not you can file for divorce benefits and doing so will NOT reduce your ex-spouse's benefit, so talk to your adviser to find out if you qualify.

---

*Fast Fact: Women make up 96% of Social Security survivor beneficiaries.[57]*

---

That was just a lot of information to digest. Social Security is a bigger bite to chew than many people think. But you don't have to figure this out alone. We have done this countless times with successful results. We have the tools. We have the experience. When we sit down with our clients, we are always working toward creating a *clear path* to retirement. That means simplifying the process, gathering as much information as we can, and creating an efficient plan.

---

[56] Social Security Administration, Understanding Benefits, 2023 https://www.ssa.gov/pubs/EN-05-10024.pdf Accessed 1/11/2023.

[57] Center on Budget and Policy Priorities, Policy Basics: Top Ten Facts about Social Security, updated March 2022, https://www.cbpp.org/research/social-security/top-ten-facts-about-social-security Accessed 1/11/2023.

Retirement is about generating income, but it is also about having an effective plan. Sometimes taking Social Security as soon as possible is the right choice. Sometimes waiting a year and withdrawing tax-free money from capital gains on non-qualified accounts makes more sense, because that would allow your benefit to grow another year. Sometimes waiting until you are age 70 is the right move. We don't know until we take a look at your goals and your situation. The point is that we look at your whole situation from an income and tax standpoint and get all the gears working and turning together toward the same goals.

## The ClearPath:

Sock market volatility, fluctuating interest rates, an unreliable bond market, inflation, and other factors have put a lot of pressure on individual portfolios to perform reliably to generate retirement income. If you are at or near retirement, it's imperative that you test the efficiency of your plan against any unnecessary drains. This includes opportunities to optimize your Social Security benefit.

### Optimize Your Social Security Benefit.
- Work with an adviser who is qualified and knowledgeable to get you a filing strategy.
- Remember, your Social Security benefit filing decision doesn't happen in a vacuum. The choice you make will affect all the other aspects of your portfolio.
- Ask for your customized Social Security timing report.

# Chapter Five

## TAXES IN RETIREMENT

*"Organizing is what you do before you do something, so that when you do it, it is not all mixed up."*

~ A. A. Milne

Since retirement is about preserving and distributing your money back to yourself in the form of income, it stands that you want to keep as much of your money away from Uncle Sam as you can. We all have to pay taxes, but there's nothing wrong with paying as little as legally possible. This is so important to us that we spend more time as advisers looking at the tax planning portion of retirement plans than we do on market allocations. If that sounds crazy, then we have some more educating to do. The fact is, you can often save more money by reducing your tax bill than you can by trying to earn more in the market. When you retire, a dollar saved truly is a dollar earned.

    Tax planning in retirement is important to us because it is an area where we see huge potential for increasing net worth. When you retire, you are no longer in your accumulation phase of life. You have already made most of the money you are going to make. Instead of chasing returns and trying to get as much growth as possible, it is time to keep as much of what you have earned as you can. One of the most effective ways of doing that is by reducing your tax bill and building tax efficiency into your income withdrawal strategy.

Here's an exercise we walk people through when introducing the concept of tax planning:

Imagine that you have three piles of money: a small, a medium, and a large pile. Say you need $15,000 per year to fill your income gap in the year that you retire. Now ask yourself, which account do you take the money from? Most people choose to take from the biggest account first. It seems like common sense—it has the most money in it and should be able to last longer. But take a moment and think about what your largest pile of retirement money is. If you are like most people, your biggest account is your 401(k) or IRA. In other words, it is qualified money, which is subject to regular income tax brackets and tax rates. It is a big pile of taxable money and withdrawing from it for income without making a plan or having a strategy could lead to higher-than-necessary taxes for you to deal with right out of the gate when you retire.

It's easy to understand why saving in a tax-deferred account is a good deal. You receive the immediate benefit of lower income taxes while also saving for retirement. Meanwhile, the money grows. In tax-deferred accounts such as your IRA, 401(k), 403(b) or TSP, you don't have to pay income taxes on the money you put in or on the interest earned until you spend it. So the money just grows and grows.

The problem? **You're also growing a future tax bill.**

Once you reach the age of 59 ½, you're able to withdraw the funds from these tax-deferred accounts without penalty. That's when the taxes finally come due—when you take this money out. So, assuming a 24 percent tax rate and a $1 million account, you don't really have $1 million to spend. In reality, you only have $760,000 or $680,000 or even $650,000 depending on your tax bracket because a certain percentage of every dollar belongs to Uncle Sam. And if history repeats itself and tax rates go up, you might even have less.

We know that tax laws and rates change over time. **We know what the tax rates are now, but we don't know where they will be in the future**. All signs point to the probability of rising taxes. The more you can reduce your tax liability now, the less income your portfolio has to generate in the future to support your lifestyle—meaning you can assume less risk with the same outcome.

It doesn't take a whole lot of brains to look at your portfolio only in terms of the rate of return and how much it can *earn*. The real test is understanding how to think like a tax planner by looking at your portfolio in terms of **how much money you get to *keep***.

---

**Fast Fact**: *Income taxes can be your single largest expense in retirement.*[58]

---

[58] FINRA, Taxation of Retirement Income, 2023, https://www.finra.org/investors/learn-to-invest/types-investments/retirement/managing-retirement-income/taxation-retirement-income Accessed 1/31/2023.

## Tax Me Now, Tax Me Later, Tax Me Some, Tax Me Never

There are four types of money when it comes to your retirement savings. For the purposes of this chapter, we are also including Social Security in the equation because it is a tax-advantaged source of income. By learning how to keep below certain income thresholds, you can learn how to diversify your retirement income from a tax standpoint to maximize your tax-advantaged income and keep more of your money.

### Taxable

You will pay taxes every year on the money inside taxable accounts. This income is reported as dividend or interest income on your 1099 tax form. Most people have at least some money in taxable accounts. Examples of these accounts include your savings, money market savings account, bank CDs, individual bonds, individual stocks, and brokerage accounts that are *not* retirement accounts. This money has essentially already passed through a tax filter—you have already paid Social Security, Medicare, state, and federal taxes on it before it hits your account. This money can be uniquely beneficial if it has experienced capital gains, which are taxed at a lower rate than ordinary income.

The drawback of taxable accounts is that you must pay taxes on any interest earned even if you don't plan to spend the money. For example, if your bank CD earned 2 percent for the year, but you're in a five-year contract, you would still owe taxes on the amount of interest earned before the CD matures. This can eat into your profits, making it difficult to keep up with inflation, particularly with bank products. If you have too much money in taxable accounts, then you might want to work with a knowledgeable tax professional who can help you do tax *planning* rather than simply tax *paying*.

---

**Fast Fact**: As of September 2022, Americans held an estimated $6.3 trillion in untaxed wealth inside their 401(k) and $11 trillion inside their IRAs.[59]

---

## Tax-Deferred

Tax-deferred accounts are sometimes called qualified accounts. Why? Because they qualify for a certain kind of tax treatment. This deal allows you to save the money *before* the income has been taxed, allowing it to grow tax-deferred until you go to spend it *later*. If you're participating in your company's retirement plan such as 401(k) or Thrift Savings Plan, 403(b), 457, IRA, SEP IRA, Simple IRA, Spousal IRA, or profit-sharing plans, then congratulations, you will qualify for retirement taxes.

These taxes come due when you take this money out. If you don't need the money right away and you keep growing it, this could cause a lot of problems later such as a higher tax rate, a bigger tax bill, a smaller amount of Social Security income, and a hike to your Medicare premiums.

The tax-deferred retirement accounts listed above all have required minimum distributions—known as the RMD—that become due once you reach a certain age. The age of this RMD has changed twice with the passing of the SECURE Act, first to age 72, and now as of January 2023, to age 73.[60] Because of the SECURE Act 2.0, the RMD will

---

[59] Investment Company Institute, 401(k) Resource Center, ICI Global, September 2022, https://www.ici.org/401k Accessed 5/18/2023.

[60] Senate Finance Committee, SECURE 2.0 Act of 2022 Title I, Jan 2023, https://www.finance.senate.gov/imo/media/doc/Secure%202.0_Section%20by%20Section%20Summary%2012-19-22%20FINAL.pdf Accessed 1/4/2023.

eventually become age 75 by the year 2033.[61] This is the age at which you must take this money out, but there's no law that says you can't take it out earlier.

**If this account grows too large, future withdrawals (or even just your RMD obligations) could drive you into higher tax brackets** which may have multiple and unintended tax consequences.

---

*Fast Fact:* Between the ages of 59½ and 73, there is no rule that restricts how much or how little you must take out of your tax-deferred retirement account.[62]

---

### Tax-Advantaged and Tax-Free

Tax-advantaged accounts give you tax-preferential treatment on your retirement income while tax-free accounts give you tax-free income. We call tax-free and tax-advantaged money the holy grail, because it gives you tax-free income from your principal *and* the gains it earns.

Everybody gets some form of tax-advantaged income during retirement thanks to Social Security. At least 15 percent of this income will be paid to you tax-free, and some people receive all of this income tax-free. How much of your Social Security income will be taxed depends on your **combined income**.

---

[61] Ibid.

[62] IRS, When Can a Retirement Plan Distribute Benefits? April 2023, https://www.irs.gov/retirement-plans/plan-participant-employee/when-can-a-retirement-plan-distribute-benefits Accessed 6/21/2023.

All Roth IRA accounts will give you tax-free retirement income. This is because the money is taxed when it's going in, so it won't be taxed again when it's coming out. **Every dollar you take out of a Roth will cost you zero dollars in taxes.** With a Roth, even the gains earned by the money comes to you tax-free, which is why many people consider doing a Roth conversion. Every dollar you convert from a traditional IRA into a Roth IRA will come back to you in the form of tax-free retirement income. Additionally, if any of the money you have in a Roth IRA passes to your beneficiaries, then they will be able to enjoy it tax-free for 10 years.

Here is the cliff-notes version to make this easier to remember:

Taxable accounts = tax me now.
Tax-deferred accounts = tax me later.
Tax-advantaged = tax me some.
Tax-free accounts = tax me never.

---

**Fast Fact:** *About 40% of people who get Social Security have to pay income taxes on their benefits.*[63]

---

[63] SSA "Social Security Administration: Retirement Benefits" 2023 https://www.ssa.gov/pubs/EN-05-10035.pdf Page 11 Accessed 4/20/2023.

## How Your Social Security Benefit Is Taxed

Learning how to optimize your Social Security benefit plays a big role in gaining a tax-efficient withdrawal strategy. Because the income thresholds for this benefit haven't changed since 1980, most people will be taxed on this benefit. But there are ways to mitigate the bite, and with proper planning, it might even be possible to receive more of this income tax-free.

**As little as 15 percent and as much as 100 percent of your Social Security income can be received tax-free.** Up to 85 percent of your benefit may be taxed, and it will be taxed at your highest marginal income tax rate. This came as a big surprise to Karl and Sheila.

*Karl and Sheila retired with a provisional income of $90,000 a year. Their income included Karl's pension of $40,000 a year, Sheila's RMD of $30,000 a year, and one-half of their combined Social Security benefits at $20,000.*

*Karl and Sheila's provisional income exceeded the $44,000 threshold, so 85 percent of their Social Security benefits were taxed at their highest marginal tax rate. Because they were in the 22 percent tax bracket, and 85 percent of their Social Security benefit was $34,000, they were paying $7,480 a year in taxes on their Social Security income.*

*However, there was an unintended side effect of this. Karl and Sheila were receiving $7,480 less in income each year! To make up for this and so they could meet their expenses, Beverly withdrew more money from the IRA. At a 22 percent tax rate, she took out $9,589 to compensate for the taxation.*

*Had that $9,589 been allowed to stay in the IRA, it would have continued to grow tax-deferred. Every year as the cost-of-living adjustment goes up, they get an increased* tax bill, requiring more and more money to come out of the IRA. Over time, this could easily amount to anywhere from $300,000 to $1 million in lost assets due to Social Security taxation.[64]

Karl and Sheila need a better plan.

The two things to know when determining how your Social Security benefit will be taxed are your *provisional income* and your *income threshold*. Let's take a look at each of these key areas.

## PROVISIONAL INCOME FORMULA

The magic formula for figuring your combined income is the total of three things:

1. **Your adjusted gross income.** This includes income from your job, rental income, royalties, interest, dividend payments, business income, alimony payments, pensions, and annuities. This does NOT include your Social Security income.
2. **Your non-taxable interest income.** This includes any sources of tax-free interest income such as tax-exempt bond funds and municipal bonds.
3. **Half of your Social Security income.** This is where you add your Social Security income, but only HALF of this income is counted. The formula looks like this:

Your adjusted gross income + any non-taxable Interest Income
+ ½ of your Social Security income
=
Your provisional income

---

[64] The above story is a fictional story using actual figures from sources believed to be reliable. This example is shown for illustrative purposes only. Estimated projections do not represent or guarantee the actual results of any transaction, and no representation is made that any transaction will, or is likely to, achieve results similar to those shown.

## INCOME THRESHOLD

The Social Security Administration bases the amount of your taxation on *income thresholds* dependent on your filing status. These are set by law and not adjusted annually.

The following income thresholds are current as of 2023.[65] **If you file a federal tax return as an "individual"** and your *provisional income* is:
- less than $25,000, then you may pay zero taxes on your Social Security benefit.
- between $25,000 and $34,000, then you may have to pay income tax on up to 50 percent of your benefits.
- more than $34,000, then you may have to pay income tax on up to 85 percent of your benefits.

**If you file a joint return,** and you and your spouse have a *provisional income* that is:
- less than $32,000, then you may pay zero taxes on your Social Security benefit.
- between $32,000 and $44,000, then you may have to pay income tax on up to 50 percent of your benefits.
- more than $44,000, then you may have to pay income tax on up to 85 percent of your benefits.

**If you are married and file a separate tax return,** then you probably will pay taxes on your benefits.

Another complication is the addition of taxes at the state level. There are a handful of states that tax your Social Security income, however, some of them make special provisions. For example, Missouri, West Virginia, and Vermont only tax benefits if your income exceeds

---

[65] SSA. "Retirement Benefits." https://www.ssa.gov/benefits/retirement/planner/taxes.html. Accessed 1/11/2023.

certain (generous) thresholds, and Utah allows a tax credit for a portion of the benefits, beginning in 2021.

Your adviser should keep track of the changing rules for your state. For your 2022 tax return, the 12 states that tax Social Security income are, in alphabetical order: Colorado, Connecticut, Kansas, Minnesota, Missouri, Montana, Nebraska, New Mexico, Rhode Island, Utah, and Vermont.[66]

---

**Fast Fact**: *Studies find that a more tax-efficient withdrawal strategy can help boost your nest egg anywhere from 1 to 11%.[67]*

---

## Get A Withdrawal Strategy

Once you're retired and living off your benefits and the money in your various accounts, you have a choice:
1. Withdraw this money willy-nilly with a tax-inefficient strategy.
2. Follow conventional wisdom and put off spending those tax-deferred dollars for as long as possible.
3. Work with an adviser who specializes in retirement distribution strategies to get a customized withdrawal strategy.

Obviously, no one wants to run out of money before running out of life. Yet most people choose option two because they want to put off the odious task of paying taxes for as long as possible. Really, who can blame you?

---

[66] Mengle, Rocky, and Block, Sandy, 12 States That Tax Social Security Benefits, Kiplinger, November 2022, https://www.kiplinger.com/retirement/social-security/603803/states-that-tax-social-security-benefits Accessed 1/11/2023.

[67] Geisler, Greg; Harden, Bill; Hulse, David S., A Comparison of the Tax Efficiency of Decumulation Strategies, Financial Planning Association (FPA), March 2021, https://www.financialplanningassociation.org/article/journal/MAR21-comparison-tax-efficiency-decumulation-strategies Accessed 1/11/2023.

And yet, the Journal of Financial Planning finds that for most retirees, **a more tax-efficient withdrawal strategy can help boost your nest egg anywhere from 1 to 11 percent when compared to conventional wisdom or non-customized strategies.**[68] For some people, this might include waiting to file for Social Security, allowing this tax-advantaged source of income to grow as big as possible, while spending those tax-deferred accounts now while taxes are effectively on sale. For other people, it might include Roth conversions to take full advantage of your low tax-brackets during the early years of retirement.

The optimal approach must be tailored to your situation, but the rewards can increase how long your wealth will last in retirement.

How much longer?

That same study in the Journal of Financial Planning found that tax-efficient withdrawal strategies can **add years of life to your portfolio without assuming additional risk.**[69]

---

*Fast Fact: Studies find that 40% of wealthy households—defined as having a combined income from Social Security and savings averaging $7,242 a month—are at risk of not being able to maintain their lifestyle due to taxation.*[70]

---

[68] Geisler, Greg; Harden, Bill; Hulse, David S., A Comparison of the Tax Efficiency of Decumulation Strategies, Financial Planning Association (FPA), March 2021, https://www.financialplanningassociation.org/article/journal/MAR21-comparison-tax-efficiency-decumulation-strategies Accessed 5/4/2023.

[69] Ibid.

[70] Chen, Anqi, and Munnell, Alicia H., How Much Taxes Will Retirees Owe On Their Retirement Income? Center for Retirement Research at Boston College, November 2020, Page 15, https://crr.bc.edu/wp-content/uploads/2020/11/wp_2020-16..pdf Accessed 5/04/2023.

## The ClearPath:

You can't control the tax rates and brackets, but you can control how you withdraw your money in order to maximize your net income. Taking money from your biggest pile of money to pay your lifestyle expenses may seem like it makes the most sense, but you don't know what the most tax-efficient withdrawal strategy is until you consider all your options. A better plan is to work with an adviser who can help you customize a withdrawal strategy that takes your exact tax situation into account.

### Get A Tax-Efficient Withdrawal Strategy

- Identify how much of your future retirement income is in tax-deferred accounts.
- Get a tax-efficient claiming strategy for your Social Security.
- Investigate how you can withdrawal your money to reduce your exposure to higher taxes in the future.

# Chapter Six

## ROTH IRA CONVERSIONS: WHEN DOES IT MAKE SENSE?

*"You cannot make progress without making decisions."*

~ Jim Rohn

The goal of tax planning in retirement is to pay as little in taxes as you can. There are a lot of things that make this a complicated process, but that's the gist of it. This feels good for obvious reasons, but it also helps take the stress off your portfolio. By keeping more of your money in your pocket, you don't need to rely on growth and gains as much, which can give you the freedom to take on less risk with your money when generating the income.

One way of minimizing your tax bill is by spending as much as you can within your current tax bracket without bumping up to a higher one. This allows you to take advantage of the highest amount of cashflow within a tax bracket as possible while paying the lowest rate possible. If you don't need all the income, there is another option for what you can do with that extra money. You've guessed it: a Roth conversion. This chapter will show you how you may be able to leverage today's tax laws to help protect your investments from being overtaxed.

While it was Benjamin Franklin who said nothing is certain except death and taxes, you might extend this to say, *"increasing* taxes." This could also be true of your IRA because of required minimum distribution (RMD) withdrawal rules.

Even if you don't want to spend this money, even if you have plans to leave your IRA to your wife or family or a charity, the rules for IRA distributions say you MUST spend this money. As you age, the IRS *increases* the amount you must withdrawal because getting older means you have less time to spend it. So as your account gets bigger and you grow older, you'll be required to spend more of this money even if you don't want to.

This will theoretically mean an increasing tax bill because your income will increase. This can also trigger a higher marginal tax rate, a reduction in the amount of Social Security income you get to keep, and an increase to your Medicare Parts B and D.

There is good news, however. This is one area of your retirement plan where *you have more control than you think.*

## The Window Of Tax Opportunity

Let's not confuse *paying* your taxes with *planning* for your taxes. Paying your taxes is what you do every year by the deadline of April 15. By then, it's usually too late to do anything but pay what you owe.

*Planning* for your taxes means looking ahead—sometimes as long as 10 years into the future—and using current tax law to your advantage.

So, looking ahead, how many people think that tax rates will be going *down* during the next 15 years?
Nobody.
How many people think taxes will be going *up*?
Everybody.
When you think about retirement spanning 20 to 30 years, and you look at where we are today as compared to where we've been, it becomes pretty obvious which direction we're headed. The question is, how high will they go?

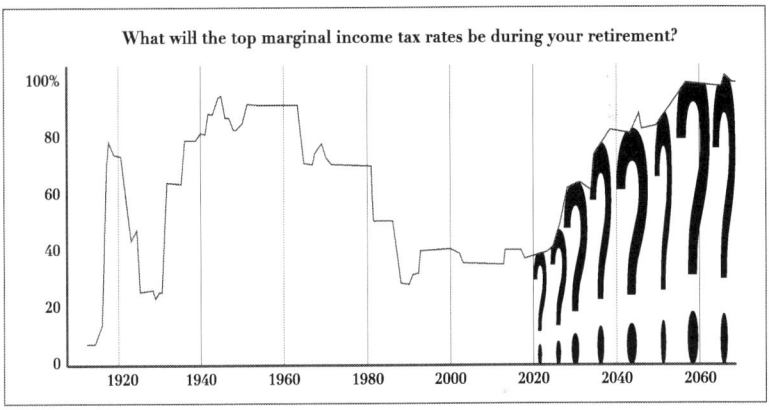

Source: Magellan Financial using data from the Urban-Brookings Tax Policy Center, "Historical Individual Income Tax Parameters: 1913 to 2018".

On November 16, 2017, the House of Representatives passed the Tax Cuts and Jobs Act to reform the individual income tax codes. This act lowered tax rates on wages, investment, and business income, and it changed the standard deductions for millions of filers, nearly doubling the standard amount. But these individual income-tax changes are set to expire on December 31, 2025, when tax brackets will revert to 2017 levels.[71] This will be a significant day for most taxpayers.

**Twenty-three provisions are set to expire, so most taxpayers will see a tax hike unless provisions are extended.**[72]

What this means for you is that right now we have a window of opportunity where it's possible to do some real planning. Taxes are at historically low levels. They aren't going to stay this low forever.

---

*Fast Fact:* The highest marginal tax rate for 2023 was at a historic low. The highest rate ever seen was 94% in 1944-1945. It remained in the 50% to 90% range until it went down in 1987 to 38.50%.[73]

---

## The Who, When, and What Of The RMD

Retirement accounts have rules about when and how much money you may put in. Some of these accounts also have rules about when and how much you must take out. The required minimum distribution (RMD) is the amount of money you are required to withdraw once you hit a certain age. What follows is the who, when, what, and why of the RMD.

**WHO:** Anyone who owns a retirement account such as a 401(k) or an IRA account that is not preceded by the words "Roth" may be required to take an RMD. This includes

---

[71] El-Sibaie, Amir, A Look Ahead at Expiring Tax Provisions, Tax Foundation, January 2018 https://taxfoundation.org/look-ahead-expiring-tax-provisions Accessed 6/23/2023.

[72] Ibid.

[73] Tax Policy Center, Historical Highest Marginal Income Tax Rates, May 2023, https://www.taxpolicycenter.org/statistics/historical-highest-marginal-income-tax-rates Accessed 6/23/2023.

traditional IRAs and IRA-based plans such as SEPs, SARSEPs, and SIMPLE IRAs. It does not apply to Roth or non-qualified accounts. It may also not apply if you are still contributing to your 401(k).

**WHEN**: When you reach a certain age, your RMD comes due. The age of this RMD has changed twice since the passing of the SECURE Act, first from age 70 ½ to age 72, and now as of January 2023, to age 73.[74] Because of the SECURE Act 2.0, the RMD will eventually become age 75 by the year 2033.[75] It's wise to expect they will continue to change every few years as people continue to live longer.

**WHAT:** To calculate the exact amount of your RMD, the IRS uses a division formula based on two things: 1) your account's balance at the end of the preceding year, and 2) the number of years that you're expected to live. Your RMD amount is then calculated by dividing your tax-deferred retirement account balance as of December 31 of last year by your life expectancy factor.

For example, if your account balance at the end of the year was $500,000 and you're expected to live another 27.4 years, then your RMD would be $18,248 for that year.

The IRS calculates your life expectancy by looking at the Uniform Lifetime Table. This table calculates the number of years that you have left to pay the taxes you owe on this amount of money. Because we're living longer, the IRS updated the tables with new rates going into effect beginning 2022. The longer you live, the shorter amount of time you have to pay the taxes owed, so the withdrawal rates (RMD%) *increase* as you age.

---

[74] Senate Finance Committee, SECURE 2.0 Act of 2022 Title I, Jan 2023, https://www.finance.senate.gov/imo/media/doc/Secure%202.0_Section%20by%20Section%20Summary%2012-19-22%20FINAL.pdf Accessed 1/4/2023.

[75] Ibid.

## UNIFORM LIFETIME TABLE

| Age | Life Expectancy Factor | RMD % | Age | Life Expectancy Factor | RMD % |
|---|---|---|---|---|---|
| 72 | 27.4 | 3.65% | 97 | 7.8 | 12.82% |
| 73 | 26.5 | 3.77% | 98 | 7.3 | 13.70% |
| 74 | 25.5 | 3.92% | 99 | 6.8 | 14.71% |
| 75 | 24.6 | 4.07% | 100 | 6.4 | 15.63% |
| 76 | 23.7 | 4.22% | 101 | 6.0 | 16.67% |
| 77 | 22.9 | 4.37% | 102 | 5.6 | 17.86% |
| 78 | 22.0 | 4.55% | 103 | 5.2 | 19.23% |
| 79 | 21.1 | 4.74% | 104 | 4.9 | 20.41% |
| 80 | 20.2 | 4.95% | 105 | 4.6 | 21.74% |
| 81 | 19.4 | 5.15% | 106 | 4.3 | 23.26% |
| 82 | 18.5 | 5.41% | 107 | 4.1 | 24.39% |
| 83 | 17.7 | 5.65% | 108 | 3.9 | 25.64% |
| 84 | 16.8 | 5.95% | 109 | 3.7 | 27.03% |
| 85 | 16.0 | 6.25% | 110 | 3.5 | 28.57% |
| 86 | 15.2 | 6.58% | 111 | 3.4 | 29.41% |
| 87 | 14.4 | 6.94% | 112 | 3.3 | 30.30% |
| 88 | 13.7 | 7.30% | 113 | 3.1 | 32.26% |
| 89 | 12.9 | 7.75% | 114 | 3.0 | 33.33% |
| 90 | 12.2 | 8.20% | 115 | 2.9 | 34.48% |
| 91 | 11.5 | 8.70% | 116 | 2.8 | 35.71% |
| 92 | 10.8 | 9.26% | 117 | 2.7 | 37.04% |
| 93 | 10.1 | 9.90% | 118 | 2.5 | 40.00% |
| 94 | 9.5 | 10.53% | 119 | 2.3 | 43.48% |
| 95 | 8.9 | 11.24% | 120 | 2.0 | 50.00% |
| 96 | 8.4 | 11.90% | | | |

Source: 2022 IRS Uniform Lifetime Table

**WHY:** Because retirement accounts are tax-deferred accounts, you deferred the taxes—meaning you didn't pay them yet. The RMD is the amount of money you must withdraw and then pay income taxes on. But perhaps the more important question to ask yourself is, "Why are we talking about this now?" We are devoting a chapter to this subject because when you do take this money out, it gets taxed as ordinary income. And that could trigger a series of ugly tax consequences.

Taking an IRA distribution no matter how big or small will increase your annual income. This has the potential to set off the following:
- An increase to your marginal tax rate.
- An increase in the amount of overall income taxes you pay.
- An increase in the amount of your Social Security benefit that is taxable.
- An increase to your Medicare Parts B and D premiums.

*How much will your taxes go up?* Crossing over the threshold into a new marginal tax rate can increase your overall tax bill by as much as 83 percent under current law, or 67 percent using 2017 tax brackets.

## Married Filing Jointly

| Old Law | | Tax Cuts & Jobs Act | |
|---|---|---|---|
| 10% | $0 - $19,050 | 10% | $0 - $19,050 |
| 15% | $19,050 - $77,400 | 12% | $19,050 - $77,400 |
| 25% | $77,400 - $156,150 | 22% | $77,400 - $165,000 |
| 28% | $156,150 - $237,950 | 24% | $165,000 - $315,000 |
| 33% | $237,950 - $424,950 | 32% | $315,000 - $400,000 |
| 35% | $424,950 - $480,050 | 35% | $400,000 - $600,000 |

⎯⎯ **67% Increase**                 **83% Increase** ⎯⎯

Source: Urban-Brookings Tax Policy Center. Recent History of the Tax Code, "How did the Tax Cuts and Jobs Act change personal taxes?"

*What's the deal with Medicare Parts B and D?* Once you become eligible for Medicare, you will pay a premium each month, automatically deducted from your Social Security. Most people pay the standard premium amount; however, if your modified adjusted gross income goes above a certain threshold—even if this is due to a one-time withdrawal—then you trigger an increase to your payment known as **IRMAA** (Income Related Monthly Adjustment Amount). This adjustment also means an increase in Medicare Part D.

    **One common trigger of IRMAA is the RMD, so make sure your adviser is aware of how much retirement income you are required to pull out.**

    *Can you take out your RMD early?* Yes. You can take out this money early before you turn age 73 and any time after you reach age 59½. You can also take MORE money out of your IRA than required by the RMD, but you can't take less. Failing to take out the full amount, or failing to withdraw the RMD by the deadline, will cost you a penalty tax of 25 percent.

> Harry had $500,000 in his IRA when he retired at the age of 63. Because he worked for the federal government, he had a pension and an amount from Social Security. He planned to leave his IRA money to his wife and family. He retired and continued to let it accumulate, leaving it in the stock market where, during the next 10 years, it grew to just over $1 million.
>
> Harry was proud of doubling the IRA, but something else happened after 10 years—Harry turned 73 years old. Now, he was required to start taking his RMD. He withdrew the required $39,000, and that was reported to the IRS as income. That pushed him into a higher income tax bracket, increasing his taxes; at the same time, he also owed more money in Social Security taxes—at the new higher rate.
>
> Harry realized he had created a tax nightmare. If he doubles his money again at the age of 83, his RMD could require that he withdraw 5.65 percent of this money based on the current life expectancy table. That income would move him up again into an even higher tax bracket, causing even more of his Social Security to be taxed, more of his pension to be taxed, and more of his IRA money to go to Uncle Sam.
>
> This is not at all what Harry had in mind when he saved this money.[76]

---

[76] The above story is a fictional story using actual figures from sources believed to be reliable. This example is shown for illustrative purposes only. Estimated projections do not represent or guarantee the actual results of any transaction, and no representation is made that any transaction will, or is likely to, achieve results similar to those shown.

## How To Get Rid Of Your RMD

The rule of 72 tells us how long it will take for your money to double given a fixed rate of interest. For example, if your account is making 6 percent with a balance of $1 million and you retire at age 61, then you're going to see that account double in 12 years. That means when you reach age 73, your RMD is going to be based on a $2 million account.

Now, take a look at the Uniform Life Expectancy table and notice how the number of years (the distribution period) keeps getting lower while the percentage of your account balance (the amount you're required to withdraw) keeps getting bigger. Mathematically speaking, if you're dividing a number that keeps getting bigger by a number that keeps getting lower, **the amount of your RMD will keep getting higher**. As you get older and need this money less, you'll be required to take out more money from an account that you'd potentially intended to leave for someone else, meanwhile triggering those ugly tax consequences.

There is a way to get rid of your RMD. If you do some thoughtful planning and take care of these pesky taxes ahead of time, you can fund an account that would allow you and your beneficiaries to withdraw contributions tax-free at any time. And once you've funded this strategy for at least five years, even the interest can be accessed without having to pay a penny in taxes.

---

*Fast Fact:* Once your RMD becomes due, for every dollar you fail to withdraw the IRS will charge a 25% penalty.[77]

---

[77] IRS, Retirement Plan and IRA Required Minimum Distributions FAQs, March 2023, https://www.irs.gov/retirement-plans/retirement-plan-and-ira-required-minimum-distributions-faqs#:~:text=the%20required%20deadline%3F-,(updated%20March%2014%2C%20 2023),timely%20corrected%20within%20two%20years Accessed 5/5/2023.

Using the marginal income tax rates as a guide and working with an adviser, it's possible to pull out a strategic amount from your IRA every year while staying below your income threshold to fund a Roth. Even if your income is higher than the maximum the IRS allows for regular Roth contributions, there is an IRS-sanctioned method for funding a Roth during retirement. Withdrawals from your IRA will be taxed as income at your current rate because a Roth is funded with post-tax money. But because Roth withdrawals are not taxed later, even on the interest they accumulate, it can be a better deal for someone in a rising-tax environment.

Roth conversions are not for everyone. They require proper tax planning and an adviser who takes a holistic approach because conversions could trigger unintended tax consequences if they are not carefully analyzed. In some cases, consulting with multiple professionals might be appropriate. This chapter is designed to help give you an education about Roth conversion benefits. When you convert to a Roth, you receive significant tax advantages:

- No RMDs.
- Tax-deferred growth.
- Tax-free interest.
- Tax-free income.
- Tax-free money to your beneficiaries.

All the money you put into a Roth can be taken out again without being reported on your 1040 tax form. Furthermore, when your account earns interest, you will not receive a 1099 form requiring you to report those gains, and even if your account doubles, you will have no RMD! All interest earned, whether it is from dividends or capital gains, are distributed tax-free as long as the account has been opened for at least five years. This is sometimes known as the "five-year rule" for the Roth IRA.

In a rising-tax environment, a Roth IRA can be a real gift to both yourself and your beneficiaries because when you go to spend this money, nothing happens! You don't owe income tax on the interest or on the money you take out, so the amount of your annual income as reported to the IRS and Social Security does not change. Your Social Security is not taxed at a higher rate, your marginal tax rate doesn't go up, and there is no change to the cost of your Medicare benefits.

---

**Fast Fact:** *For savers over the age of 50, you can now contribute an additional $7,500 to a 401(k), 403(b), or other qualified retirement plan on top of the $22,500 federal limit.*[78]

---

## The ClearPath:

A Roth conversion is a strategy to pay taxes on your tax-deferred money while you are in the lowest income tax bracket possible. You *will* have to pay taxes on this money at some point. You can do it now when you know the tax rate and can control the bracket you are in, or you can do it later when both of those things may be more out of your control. Be strategic. Even though you'll have to pay the taxes now, you'll be paying them at a known rate vs. an unknown rate that is likely to be much higher in the future.

---

[78] IRS, Retirement Topics – 401(k) and Profit-Sharing Contribution Limits, Nov 2023 https://www.irs.gov/retirement-plans/plan-participant-employee/retirement-topics-401k-and-profit-sharing-plan-contribution-limits Accessed 5/06/2023.

**Diversify Your Tax Landscape.**

- Forecast your RMD to figure out whether the income will be usable or excess.
- Open up a Roth IRA and begin funding it to get the five-year clock ticking.
- Diversify your tax landscape so that you have optimum sources of tax-free and tax-advantaged retirement income.

# Chapter Seven

## FINAL THOUGHTS

*"Prepare and prevent, don't repair and repent."*

~ Author Unknown

Now that you know it isn't about how *much* money you have, but how you *use* it when it comes to income in retirement, it's time to get organized. Instead of chasing that imaginary number, you can take stock of what you have and see how and when you might use it to accomplish your retirement goals.

Remember our three main principles:
1. Helping you see a bigger version of what is possible in retirement.
2. Helping you have fun along the way.
3. Eliminating obstacles and creating efficiencies so you can see a clear path forward to your retirement goals.

    Hopefully you can see some new possibilities for how to leverage your money instead of just siphoning off your monthly income from a big pile. Having a retirement plan that takes income, taxes, inflation, and other variables into account is called active planning. It doesn't rely on hope or luck or a good market—although those things can all help. It relies on educated decisions based on all the information available to us today. And if that information changes tomorrow, then we will change the plan accordingly.

The main takeaway here is that there isn't a single financial product or service or account or asset class that is going to solve your problems. Products don't solve problems, but plans do. A plan can give you solutions. Financial products are the tools you use to achieve your goals. You can take a look at your portfolio right now, as it stands, and ask yourself, "Why do I own the products that are in there?" Are they working together in harmony as part of a larger vision? Do you remember or know why you have selected them? What purpose are they serving? How are they helping to advance your vision of your future?

The future is full of unknowns, but here is what we do know:
- You need income to fund your retirement goals.
- The price of consumable goods and the cost of living rises over time.
- Taxes on tax-deferred money will come due during your retirement.

Without a plan, the scenario could play out something like this: you pick a date to stop working, and you file for your Social Security benefits to begin. After your last day of work, you receive your benefit check and then withdraw money from your 401(k) to meet the rest of your needs for the month. This works fine for the year you retire, and the year after that. But what happens if a year or two later the market takes a big downturn, and you are still withdrawing money from your 401(k)? What happens in 10 years if you decide you need a new roof on the house? Or if you want to help your grandkids' with their college tuition? What happens if, in 15 or 20 years, you need long-term care or assisted living? Can you afford to just keep siphoning money off your 401(k) while it is exposed to the whims of the market?

One of the misconceptions we find that people have about income in retirement is that they think their expenses will stay the same, and that is rarely the case. When you pull money from an investable asset that is going up and down with the market, over time, you will need to take more and more money because of inflation. The earning power and stability of that asset diminishes over time until it can no longer sustain itself.

### Create a ClearPath to Retirement

No two retirements are alike. Everyone has different amounts of money, different health concerns, different goals, different timelines. There are countless variables that make this time after your career unique. There is no single retirement plan or rule or strategy that is right for everyone. But there is a clear path forward for you. By identifying your vision for your retirement, and comparing your risk tolerance with your income need, we can begin to get a clear picture of where that path will lead.

One of the most poignant ways of illustrating why it is so important to customize your retirement plan to protect your money comes from a story about a man who met with us several years ago. We will call him Dave.

Dave had $1.5 million in an account that he had spent his career saving. He had done well, by his standards, and he was excited about retiring and living the good life. Things were on track, until one day he called us and said he had an investment opportunity in Mexico that could triple his money twice. It was a real estate deal that he didn't want to miss out on. We asked him some questions about it and ultimately advised against it. Dave wanted to invest $300,000 of his $1.5 million, expecting to get $2 million from his investment if it worked out. Long story short: it didn't work out. Dave and his wife can still retire, and they don't have to go back to work, but they could have had a lot more cushion and a lot more options if they had protected and preserved that $300,000 instead of throwing it away on a bad real estate deal.

The point is that when you are getting ready to retire, risks become riskier. A 10 percent loss in your portfolio is more than just a percentage loss—it equates to an actual dollar amount. Those dollars don't have the same amount of time to grow and recover like they did when you were younger, especially while you are withdrawing money for income at the same time.

### Work with an Independent Professional

A comprehensive retirement plan has a lot of moving parts. And at the same time, the best plans are the simplest and most efficient. Dialing in to that kind of balance takes more than just buying the right stocks and funding the right insurance plans. It takes experience, expertise, and an eye for how all the parts of your portfolio are interacting with one another. You can buy stocks from a broker, and insurance policies from an insurance agent. But who can you buy a retirement plan from?

The answer is that you can't *buy* a retirement plan. They don't come ready made on the shelf. But you *can* work with a financial professional who is an independent fiduciary. This type of professional doesn't advocate for any particular product or strategy. They are legally required to make recommendations that are in *your* best interest. In short, when you do well, they do well, so they are incentivized to help you make decisions that benefit you over the long term.

At ClearPath Wealth Advisors, independence is at the heart of what we do. We know that you are a unique individual, and the time and work you have put into building your retirement savings should be honored with a unique and customized plan. You have earned and saved and done well at that, but now you are facing something you have never faced before. The rules are different. The tools are different. And the stakes are higher.

The analogy we use to describe planning for retirement illustrates the importance of experience, resources, and knowledge. Have you ever seen a professional sandcastle? They are impressive and very cool. And the best builders make it look easy. So easy that many people think they could do the same thing if they had the time. It's just some sand, right? But those pros don't just use sand. They make cardboard forms that they utilize for structural elements. They have special molds for intricate areas. They have customized shaping tools that help them get just the right angles. They also have the experience and the know-how, along with the tips and tricks that come with the trade. Your bucket and shovel just isn't going to cut it compared to those guys. And that's okay! You aren't a professional sandcastle builder. And you aren't a professional retirement planner. You don't need to be. That's why you have us! We have the tips and tricks, the experience, the know-how, and the knowledge to help you build something way better than a sandcastle. We can build your financial future together.

A comprehensive retirement plan is more complicated than a sandcastle and not something that an individual should have to make for themselves. By working together with a financial professional whose goal is to *educate* you to make the best decisions by showing you all the options available, you can find the clear path forward to the retirement you have earned.

Call us at ClearPath Wealth Advisors to find the clear path forward to your retirement.
**(952) 406-8011**
www.myclearpathcfo.com

# About the Authors

## Cory Zafke

Cory Zafke is all about the big picture. After spending over a decade working for an international insurance company, he decided it was time to broaden the scope of his services. Cory wanted to work without limits to help people find the financial solutions they needed to achieve their life goals. He knew he could help people navigate the most important financial decisions of their lives if he became an independent financial adviser. After a life-changing incident, he co-founded ClearPath Wealth Advisors with his business partner, Taylor Sundeen.

Cory gets energized by talking with his clients about their lives, their hopes, and their aspirations. He likes to work side-by-side with people to create tax-efficient financial plans that allow then to realize their lifestyle goals.

Cory grew up in the White Bear Lake area of Minnesota and graduated from Saint John's University in 2002, where he played soccer and studied abroad in France. Today, Cory enjoys cooking with his kids, making soup when it's cold out, and watching the Vikings, Twins, and European Soccer on the weekends. He married his wife Jill on a beach in 2008, and they currently live in Chanhassen, Minnesota with their son, Tatum, and their two daughters, Tegan and Ryan, and their French Bulldog, Claude. They like to ride their bikes to ice cream shops and enjoy a good burger and the occasional doughnut or cupcake.

# Taylor Sundeen

Tayor Sundeen created ClearPath Wealth Advisors after accumulating over 15 years of financial services experience in the Minneapolis and St. Paul area. He earned his CFP® designation in 2011 to enhance his expertise in multiple financial planning areas from tax planning and investments to insurance and estate planning.

Taylor enjoys the day-to-day interactions he has with clients, and prides himself on creating well-versed financial plans that are customized to meet his clients' income, tax, and investment planning objectives.

Taylor grew up in Spooner, Wisconsin, and graduated from UW-Eau Claire with a double major in Finance and Marketing. He lives in Maple Grove, Minnesota with his wife, Gina, and their three children: Cody, Ariana, and Gabrielle.

# Glossary of Terms

**ACCUMULATION PHASE** – The financial phase during your working years when you are saving and growing your assets.

**BENEFICIARY** – An individual entitled to collect assets as decreed by a written, legal document.

**BUY-AND-HOLD STRATEGY** – A passive investment strategy whereby market investments are bought and then held for a long period regardless of market fluctuations, so investors capture 100 percent of market gains and 100 percent of market loss.

**COMMON STOCKS** – A market investment that profits from the future success of a business entity and gives shareholders voting rights.

**COST-OF-LIVING-ADJUSTMENT (COLA)** – Adjustments that give claimants of Social Security a way to keep pace with inflation and the rising price of goods and services.

**COMBINED INCOME** – The IRS defines combined income as your adjusted gross income, plus tax-exempt interest, plus half of your Social Security benefits.

**DELAYED RETIREMENT CREDITS (DRCs)** – Credits used to increase the amount of your Social Security benefit during the period beginning with the month you achieve full retirement age and ending with the month you turn age 70.

**DISTRIBUTION PHASE** – The financial phase during your non-working years when you are spending the assets you saved.

**DISCRETIONARY EXPENSES** – The cost of travel or dining out or other things that are nice to do or have but are not necessary for basic survival.

**FIDUCIARY** – A professional who holds a legal or ethical relationship of trust to prudently take care of money or other assets for another person.

**FIXED ANNUITY** – An annuity that promises to pay the owner fixed rate of return over a period of time.

**FULL RETIREMENT AGE (FRA)** – Also known as normal retirement age, this is the age at which you become entitled to receive your full or unreduced retired worker benefit from Social Security.

**IMMEDIATE ANNUITY** – An agreement between you and an insurance company whereby the income payments start immediately, providing a set amount of income for an established period such as 20 years or an individual's lifetime.

**INCOME GAP** – The difference between your retirement living expenses and the income from guaranteed sources such as pensions or Social Security.

**INDEXED ANNUITY** – An annuity that provides fixed principal guarantees while providing returns based on an index.

**INFLATION** – The general rate at which the price of goods and services gradually rises.

**IRMAA** – An acronym for Medicare's Income-Related Monthly Adjustment Amount, which can charge a higher premium for Medicare Parts B and D for individuals with higher incomes.

**LIFETIME INCOME STREAM** – A secure source of guaranteed income payable to you that continues paying out as long as you live.

**LIQUIDITY** – How quickly or easily you can convert an asset into cash.

**NON-DISCRETIONARY EXPENSES** – The cost of necessities such as food, clothing, or shelter required for basic survival.

**PRINCIPAL** – The base amount of money that you put into an investment.

**PRIMARY INSURANCE AMOUNT (PIA)** – The amount of money you will receive from Social Security if you file at your normal or full retirement age, rounded down to the next lower whole dollar amount.

**PROBATE** – The legal process by which the assets of the deceased are properly distributed, the objective being to ensure that the deceased's debts, taxes, and other valid claims are paid out of their estate, and the assets are distributed to the intended beneficiaries.

**RISK** – The danger or probability of loss.

**REQUIRED MINIMUM DISTRIBUTION (RMD)** – The minimum amount you must withdraw from qualified retirement accounts such as a traditional IRA by April 1 following the year you reach age 73.

**ROTH IRA** – Individual retirement arrangement made with income after the taxes have been paid where designated funds can grow tax-free with no taxes due on the interest earned if the rules for withdrawal are followed.

**SSA** – An acronym that stands for the Social Security Administration.

**TRADITIONAL IRA** – An individual retirement arrangement that provides a way to set aside money for retirement using contributions that are subtracted from your income (reducing the income taxes owed) and allowed to grow tax-free until the money is withdrawn, at which point taxes are owed on both the principal and interest earned.

**VOLATILITY** – A measure of the size and frequency of the change in stock market prices.